European Costume and Fashion 1490–1790

GERMAN-SPANISH. 1548.   PLATE XII

ARCHDUKE FERDINAND.   *J. Seisenegger*

European Costume and Fashion 1490–1790

Francis M. Kelly
and
Randolph Schwabe

DOVER PUBLICATIONS, INC.
Mineola, New York

Bibliographical Note

European Costume and Fashion: 1490–1790, first published in 2002, is an unabridged republication of the work originally published in 1929 by Charles Scribner's Sons, New York and B. T. Batsford Ltd., London, under the title *Historic Costume: A Chronicle of Fashion in Western Europe, 1490–1790*. The only significant alteration consists in reproducing the seven color plates in black and white for the Dover edition.

DOVER *Pictorial Archive* SERIES

Library of Congress Cataloging-in-Publication Data

Kelly, Francis Michael, 1879-1945.
   [Historic costume]
   Eurpean costume and fashion, 1490-1790 / Francis M. Kelly & Randolph Schwabe.
      p. cm.—(Dover pictorial archive series)
   Originally published: Historic costume : a chronicle of fashion in Western Europe, 1490–1790. 2nd ed., rev. & enl. New York : Scribner ; London : B.T. Batsford, 1929.
   Includes bibliographical references and index.
   ISBN 0-486-42322-0
   1. Costume—Europe—History. I. Schwabe, Randolph, 1855–1948. II. Title. III. Series.

GT720 .K4 2002
391'.0094—dc21

2002071624

Manufactured in the United States of America
Dover Publications, Inc., 31 East 2nd Street, Mineola, N.Y. 11501

PREFACE TO SECOND EDITION

THE gratifying reception accorded both here and in America to this book has encouraged the publishers to issue a second edition. *Historic Costume* is now presented in a revised and augmented form so far as appeared consistent with maintaining the original cost to the purchaser. Among the new illustrations introduced, the authors are indebted to the Rt. Hon. the Earl of Sandwich (owner of the original), to Mr. John Drinkwater, the author, and to the publishers, Messrs. Hodder & Stoughton, for the illustration taken from *Mr. Charles, King of England*, reproduced on p. ix. For others thanks are due to Mr. Cyril Andrade, to M. Maurice Leloir, of the Société de l'Histoire du Costume, and to the authorities of the Victoria and Albert and the London Museums.

F. M. K.
R. S.

LONDON, 1929.

V

PREFACE TO FIRST EDITION

THE bibliography of costume is on the whole fairly extensive. None the less the authors of the work here presented (who have been at pains to make themselves familiar with most, if not all, of the treatises produced in England, France, and Germany since Montfaucon, Strutt, Quicherat, Fairholt, Planché, and Weiss laid the foundations) believe there is room for yet another work, envisaging the subject from a fresh angle. Indeed, it is their conviction that hitherto little or nothing of practical value has been added to the information imparted by the pioneers referred to, whose successors have been little more than *camouflés* copyists.

We are convinced from personal experience that the gradual development of fashionable attire and its accessories, the details of cut and proportion *that differentiate one decade from another*, yet need to be pointed out. One finds that, when it is desired to turn one's information to practical account in reconstructing scenes of the past, innumerable minor problems present themselves which the usual costume-book does not provide for. Accordingly, the authors have based themselves first and last on contemporary witnesses, pictorial and literary. Eschewing all irrelevant graces of style, they have sought to give, in a compact and handy form, a reliable guide to the modes of the past. It is for this reason, and because the book is *primarily* intended as a practical guide for the artist, actor, film producer, etc., that they have refrained from quoting or referring to contemporary texts. These, however, have been carefully consulted in the originals wherever possible.

The reader may be surprised at the narrow limits

PREFACE

within which the subject has been confined. The reasons are fully explained in the INTRODUCTION, and even within these limits the subject is far from being exhausted. Should the present work find favour with the public, the authors may be encouraged to follow it with a kindred work or works detailing the military, ecclesiastical, official, and professional costume of Western Europe over the same period; to say nothing of robes of state, knightly habits, liveries, and peasant-dress. The Middle Ages, too, await similar treatment.

Any measure of success the present work may attain must be largely due to the generosity of Sir Robert and Lady Witt,[1] whose wonderful library, unreservedly placed at the authors' disposal, has proved a never-failing stand-by. Moreover, the opportunity is welcomed of returning sincere thanks to the Rt. Hon. the Earl Spencer, C. F. Bell, Esq. of the Ashmolean, the late A. Wertheimer, Esq., and the proprietors of *Country Life* for supplying respectively, with leave to reproduce, the photos for Plates XVIII., XXI. B, XLII. and XVI. B.; as also to the *Connoisseur*, the *Burlington Magazine*, and the British and Victoria and Albert Museums for the use of various blocks for the plates. For leave to print Plates XXV. and XXXII. we are indebted to His Grace the Duke of Devonshire. Our thanks are also due to Mr. H. M. Cundall, I.S.O., F.S.A., for permitting us to use the blocks of " A View of Buckingham House " (Plate LXIII.), from his *History of British Water Colour Painting*.

Finally, all thanks are due to Messrs. B. T. Batsford, Ltd., who have spared no pains to send forth this book in attractive guise.

F. M. K.
R. S.

LONDON, *January* 1925.

---

[1] We are authorised to state (a fact that cannot be too widely known) that this unique collection of carefully classified photographs and reproductions of pictures and drawings, numbering well over 250,000 examples, may be freely consulted by all *bona fide* students of Art, for whose use it is expressly designed.

CONTENTS

		PAGE
PREFACE TO SECOND EDITION	. . . .	v
PREFACE TO FIRST EDITION.	. . . .	vi
INTRODUCTION		x
CHRONOLOGICAL TABLE OF ENGLISH AND FRENCH RULERS		xv

I. THE ITALIANATE TENDENCY (1490–1510) . . . I
Influence of the Italian wars on male dress—Variegated, tight hose—Small caps—Broad toes—*Décolletage*—Women's "conventual" fashions—Beginnings of the "gable" and French hoods.

II. PUFFS AND SLASHES : THE GERMAN ELEMENT (1510–1545) 29
Upper and nether stocks—Flat caps for men—Jerkins with pleated skirts—Short doublets—Splayed-out toes—Slashing of sleeves and on thighs—Points as fastenings and as ornaments—Development of the women's hoods—Women's gowns with funnel-like sleeves turned up at elbow.

III. SPANISH BOMBAST (1545–1620) 54
Universal padding, busks and tight lacing—Trunk-hose—Ruffs, bands and whisks—The farthingale.

IV. LONG LOCKS, LACE AND LEATHER (1620–1655) . . 121
The rise and decay of the "Van Dyke" fashions—The vogue of the boot—And of lace and linen—The fashion of long locks—Buff-coats.

V. EFFECTS OF THE "GRAND RÈGNE" (1655–1715) . . 157
The reign of ribbon—Rise of the periwig—Origin of modern men's suits—Cravats—The *steinkirk*—The *fontange* or commode—The apron, muff, parasol, etc.—The bustle—The apron.

VI. PANIERS, POWDER AND QUEUE (1715–1790) . . 199
The vogue of powder and queue—The wide-skirted coat transformed into a tail-coat—The bag, pigtail and catogan—The *Maccaronies*—The stock—Decline of powder—Re-appearance of the hoop—Dairymaid fashions—The bustle again—Monstrous coiffures—The sack or *robe à la française*—The polonaise—The *caraco*—The calash and *thérèse*.

PATTERNS	269
COSTUMES	279
ADDENDA	289
BIBLIOGRAPHY	293
INDEX AND GLOSSARY	297

From MS. *Journal* of the Earl of Sandwich.

The habitt taben up by d King Clerus of England
Nourub.r 1666. w.ch They Calla Vest.

VEST "AFTER THE PERSIAN MODE," FROM *Mr. Charles, King of England*,
BY JOHN DRINKWATER; HODDER & STOUGHTON.

INTRODUCTION

" Le portrait de Mme. Récamier sous sa chlamyde transparente n'est-i pas infiniment plus instructif que toutes les documentations écrites ? "—GEORGES CAIN.

IN the above quotation is largely embodied the principle governing the present work, namely, the superior lucidity of *graphic* evidence over *written*. In respect of form and proportion the slightest competent sketch is generally worth pages of description. The writer is the last man to underrate the witness of contemporary texts *when verified at first hand* ; but a nice appreciation of their precise import often tests all the skill and experience of the practised expert. It is not for the casual student nor—unless he proposes to specialise in this line for years—for the tyro. On the other hand, the endless store of really first-class *graphic* evidence, hitherto scarcely tapped for purposes of costume-study, is readily available on every side and requires comparatively little familiarity for its correct interpretation. And why—as has up to now been the practice of "costume treatises" in this country—rest content with the crude and inadequate wood-blocks of Planché and Fairholt on the one hand, on the other with "original" or "improved" drawings by modern artists? Why, in particular, should the present-day artist, when he wishes to delineate the past, base his work on somebody else's personal interpretation of the same ? What we require for reference are facsimile reproductions (or, failing that, faithful copies) of the old pictures, prints, sculptures, etc. "Reconstructions" should be only presented in serious works side by side with the originals on which they are based. Such originals, often of the finest evidential

x

INTRODUCTION

value, exist in endless variety and their realism is not seldom photographic.

While it is hoped a sufficiency of matter has been here collected to illustrate the book in a general way, it is obviously impossible, within reasonable limits, to include a tithe of what is available. The student who extends his familiarity along these lines with costume as depicted in its own day will not easily exhaust his subject. For the sake of comprehensiveness, combined with a moderate compass, we have for the present limited ourselves arbitrarily to the period of 1490–1790 : that is (roughly speaking), from the great days of early Transatlantic Exploration to the French Revolution. If any justification of this choice be required, we might point out that throughout this period paintings, prints, and sculpture supply us with evidence remarkable for its abundance, variety, and quality, supplemented by medals, tapestry, and even actual relics of old costume.

Again, for the sake of completeness within our limits, *fashionable civil apparel* alone has been dealt with ; adequately to treat of costumes military, ecclesiastical, official, professional, and rustic would have carried us far beyond the scale we had contemplated. Leaving these on one side, a few general remarks may be opportune. It should ever be borne in mind that broad periods—how much more (*pace* the usual handbooks) mere reigns—overlapped. Even till mid-Victorian days the conservatism of staider folk, worthy cits, remote provincial gentry and the *laudatores temporis acti* clung sometimes for nigh on a generation to modes obsolete in the " smart set." England, too, was apt to lag somewhat behind the Continent. On the other hand, in many instances there was a tendency to make a show of being " in the fashion," often far beyond one's real estate. Sumptuary laws only existed to be broken ; in outward show Jack would be as good—or better—than his master.

It will, we think, be found that the attentive eye soon

INTRODUCTION

learns to distinguish in ancient art between " fancy dress " and a realistic portrayal of fashion. Lely, to take but one artist, does not invite entire confidence as a faithful witness to the feminine fashions of his day. Van Dyck and Reynolds, even, are not always realists.

" Western Europe " in the text includes England, France, and the Low Countries, within which area, in the period in question, the modish forms of dress were broadly the same ; but other countries have been turned to account where their fashions inspired or accorded with those of these countries.

It should be noted how much variety of effect was obtained, particularly in the sixteenth century, by varying the draping of a cloak, leaving portions of the attire unfastened, etc. Also how varied were the methods of fastening-up garments ; thus—(1) buttons and button-holes, (2) buttons and loops, (3) lacing, (4) tying together with " points," (5) hooks and eyes. Mark, too, the varied *positions* of the openings.

The patterns of ornament, embroidery, brocades, etc., are highly characteristic of their periods and repay study. Colour is best studied in paintings and actual old textiles.

Admirable collections of old costumes are to be seen in the Victoria and Albert and in the London Museums. In the former, however, they are shown to such disadvantage as largely to discount their educational value.

None but the intending specialist can be advised to accumulate, compare, and study the old texts, but *he* will be increasingly rewarded by finding how graphic and documentary evidence cast reciprocal light one upon another.

While there is a tendency among many writers to overstate the effects of social and political conditions as reflected in contemporary fashions, there can be no doubt that dress is to some extent influenced thereby. It must not, however, be forgotten how great a part is and always has been played by caprice, snobbery, and the craving for novelty. The introductory paragraphs of the several chapters summarise briefly the tendencies of each epoch. Thus the wave of humanism and the reaction against the mediæval struggles between the great feudal lords favoured Italianate leanings. The power of the Empire and the prominence of German and Swiss mercenaries in the Italian wars gave a Teutonic turn to civilization (to say nothing of the Reformation and the prosperity of the great German cities). Spain's commanding position in European politics, her alliance with the house of Austria, and her rule in the Low Countries and parts of Italy made the verdingale, trunk-hose, and ruff typical of late sixteenth century fashion. " Cavalier " dress, graceful and unconstrained, was a protest against Spanish artificiality, and the Thirty Years' War introduced an element of the military. " Restoration " modes are a reaction against Puritanism. The gay dress of Molière's exquisites (itself an escape from the parsimony of Mazarin's regime) gives way to the pompous formalism of Mme. de Maintenon's days, from which again the light and dainty modes of the *Régence* represent an escape. Economic necessity at times plays its part as do national upheavals, of course ; but there is, perhaps, a tendency to lay more stress upon this than facts will warrant.

NOTE

So far as appeared practicable, we have endeavoured to eschew too liberal a use of technical terms and archæological discussions, aiming rather at plain statement than antiquarian pedantry. None the less we have devoted many years to extensive study of texts, and trust no statement in this work has been made without the support of testimony, both pictorial *and literary*, of the period concerned. The chief difficulties which at the outset baffle the *textual* inquirer are :

(*a*) The changes of meaning of a particular term at successive dates, and *per contra* the varied names given at divers periods to an article essentially one and the same. Readers of Charles Buttin's *Le Guet de Genève* will realise this.

(*b*) Too literal a faith in satirists' exaggerations.

(*c*) The tendency to forget that the old writer recked only of his own age and its accepted standard, and is seldom concerned with subtle distinctions. Epithets like " wide," " long," " round," etc., can only be assessed at their true value if we can gauge his conventional standards. Never disdain truisms ; they often hold the solution.

INTRODUCTION

It is important to verify dates, especially those on prints, which are often very misleading. Old plates and blocks were repeatedly used with little or no alteration, regardless of changed fashions. Thus the miscalled " James I." which forms the frontispiece of the anonymous " Jewel for Gentry " (1614) is taken *tel quel* from Turberville's *Book of Hawking* (1575). Again, Crispin de Passe's famous plates to Pluvinel's treatise on horsemanship,[1] published 1623-4, were actually executed in 1617. As an example of provincial conservatism we may cite the effigy in Gloucester Cathedral of Abraham Blackleech (*d.* 1639), whose costume is *entirely* after the fashion of 1625-30.

[1] Pluvinel died in 1620.

CHRONOLOGICAL TABLE OF ENGLISH
AND FRENCH RULERS, 1490–1790

HENRY VII.	.	1485–1509	CHARLES VIII.	.	1483–1498
HENRY VIII.	.	1509–1547	LOUIS XII. .	.	1498–1515
EDWARD VI.	.	1547–1553	FRANCIS I. .	.	1515–1547
MARY . .	.	1553–1558	HENRY II. .	.	1547–1559
ELIZABETH .	.	1558–1603	FRANCIS II. .	.	1559–1560
JAMES I. .	.	1603–1625	CHARLES IX.	.	1560–1574
CHARLES I. .	.	1625–1649	HENRY III. .	.	1574–1589
COMMONWEALTH	.	1649–1660	HENRY IV. .	.	1589–1610
CHARLES II. .	.	1660–1685	LOUIS XIII.	.	1610–1643
JAMES II. .	.	1685–1688	LOUIS XIV. .	.	1643–1715
WILLIAM III.	.	1688–1702	LOUIS XV. .	.	1715–1774
ANNE . .	.	1702–1714	(REGENCY .	.	1715–1723)
GEORGE I. .	.	1714–1727	LOUIS XVI. .	.	1774–1793
GEORGE II. .	.	1727–1760			
GEORGE III..	.	1760–1820			

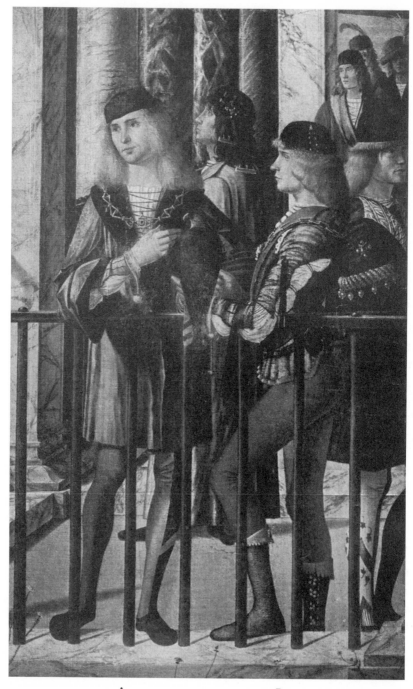

A   B

LEGEND OF ST. URSULA (DETAIL).   *Carpaccio.*

HISTORIC COSTUME

I

THE ITALIANATE TENDENCY (1490-1510)

AFTER mediæval ideals had received their death-blow—on the Continent with Charles the Bold's overthrow at Nancy in 1477, in England on Bosworth Field in 1485—the Italian campaigns of the French kings, Charles VIII. and Louis XII., contributed powerfully to the diffusion of Italian Renaissance culture throughout Western Europe. With regard to costume, the new movement, which chiefly affected men's fashions, may be said to be definitely established by 1490. Italianate influences are perceptible in female attire, but in the main they are counteracted by a strong Franco-Flemish tradition. A prevalent nun-like character in women's dress at this date has earned it the name of the " conventual " style.

MEN

BODY GARMENTS.—Costume was comparatively simple in its main lines. The high-shouldered jackets of the late Gothic period, with long narrow waists, pleated backs and high collars, went out of fashion. The high collar, open in front, is rare after 1500.

To distinguish with precision the various body garments worn would require an analytical essay on a scale disproportionate to this book, and even then would leave many points open to question. For simplicity, we propose four categories :

(i) The *doublet*, close fitting and relatively short—the prototype of the modern waistcoat. It may be regarded as a sleeved garment, though the sleeves appear often to have been detachable.

(ii) The *jerkin* or jacket, worn *over* the doublet, more or less shaped to the figure, sometimes rather loose, and with skirts of varying length.

(iii) The *gown*, cut very full and long, and open in front. It might be confined by a girdle at the waist.

(iv) The *cloak*, of varying shape and length. Either the gown or the cloak might be worn over the doublet and jerkin combined.

To clear the ground for subsequent matter we must here point out certain difficulties. The presence of a different material at the openings of a garment, or the use of visible undersleeves, does not necessarily postulate the existence of a complete undergarment, any more than the modern " dickey " and detachable linen cuffs prove the presence of a white shirt. Not only were sleeves detachable and changeable, but small pieces of material—" fore-parts," " stomachers," " fore-sleeves," etc.—were commonly worn to fill certain gaps. There is even evidence of garments having two pairs of sleeves ; the uppermost, hanging loose, being uniform with the body garment, while the undersleeve, covering the arm, differed in material, pattern, or colour. Where two more or less close-fitting, shaped body garments seem indicated, we may, however, conveniently consider the outer as a *jerkin*, the inner as a *doublet*. Apart from this we will apply the latter term to a skirtless or short-skirted coat, the former to one rather fuller or with longer skirts.

There are also intermediate types between the *cloak* and the *gown*, which are difficult to place. We shall distinguish the latter principally as a garment with *practicable* sleeves or arm-holes ; the *cloak* being considered as simply draped or slung from the shoulder.

MIRACLE OF ST. GILES.   *Master of St. Giles.*

If these distinctions be conceded, we may take as instances :

Doublets.—Plates I. B ; V. C ; Figs. 2, 3 (A), 5.

Jerkins.—Plates II. B ; IV. B ; V. A and B ; Fig. I (A and B).

Gowns.—Plates I. A ; II. A ; III. ; IV. A ; Figs. I (C and D), 3 (C).

Cloaks.—Plates II. D ; V. C ; Fig. 4.

FIG. I.—Franco-Flemish. *c.* 1490–95.

From the beginning of the period the *doublet* grew steadily more and more *décolleté*. The tendency from about 1500–25 was for a square *décolletage*, but there are frequent examples of a deep V- or U-shaped opening down the breast, the gap being filled by the " waistcoat " (a short under-doublet [1]), or by the " stomacher " (a vest-piece or " front," analogous to the modern " dickey ") ; or by the

[1] The word " waistcoat," in this sense, is found in sixteenth century texts and earlier.

shirt alone (Fig. 6, c). Not unusual after 1500 is a doublet with wrap-over or double-breasted fronts (Plate IV. D; Fig. 14, B) tied or buckled at one side. *Facings*, or lapels, are more characteristic of jerkins, gowns, and cloaks than of doublets. Up to about 1510 the frontal opening was often (especially in Italy) laced across (Plate I. A, B). A seam down the centre of the back was sometimes left open to show the undergarment. Doublet sleeves were mostly close-fitting, at least from the elbow downward ; however, wide sleeves tightening at the wrist are also common (Plate IV. D ; and Fig. 2). There are many examples of

sleeves *slashed* (*vide infra*) and puffed at shoulder and elbow, or *paned* (slashed into longitudinal bands or panels) above the elbow.

The *jerkin* often had a full, long skirt puckered into formal pleats (Plates IV. B, and V. B), which might differ from the body by being made of two stuffs alternating in stripes or other combinations of colour.[1] The facings of the jerkin usually continue at the back of the neck in a broad collar, either round or square (Plate V. A, B). The

FIG. 2.—German. *c.* 1505.

sleeves might be long and full, and as often as not we find them slit lengthwise or across for the passage of the arm in its close undersleeve (Figs. I, B ; and 2). It is quite usual in the sixteenth century to find one or more such cross-slits (sometimes T- or ⊢-shaped), which allow the upper sleeve to hang free from the shoulder, elbow, or wrist. This treatment does not preclude the sleeve from being put to its proper use, " dummies " and sleeves of exaggerated length being more characteristic of ensuing periods.

The *gown* was customary for ceremonial and official

---

[1] The stripes in Plate II. B, are hardly a case in point, as they merely continue the design of the body. These pleated kilts are called *bases*.

wear, and was in general use among the staider folk; though young fops and soldiers might display themselves in jerkins and doublets, or in doublets only. It reached sometimes to the feet, sometimes to the knees, or else midway between knee and foot (Plates I. A; II. A; III.; IV. A; and Figs. I, C, D; 3, C). It was lined or faced with fur or rich materials, the collar, when there was a collar,

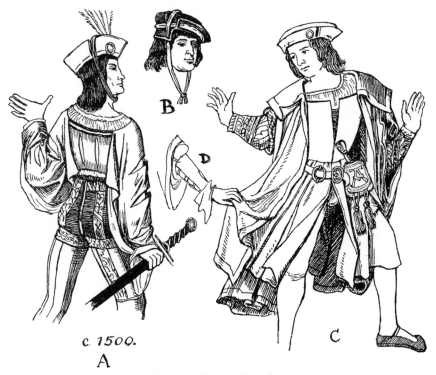

c. 1500.

A

B

D

C

FIG. 3.—Franco-Flemish.

following the forms which have been indicated in the case of the jerkin. The sleeves too, scarcely differ from those belonging to the jerkin, except in a tendency to greater fullness and length.

Cloaks varied in form and size. Plate II. D shows what is apparently a mere drapery wrapped about at the will of the wearer. The same fashion occurs in Signorelli's " Fall of Antichrist " at Orvieto (1500) and in other pictures.

There were very short circular cloaks, and probably semi-circular types as well, which were slung by a cord from one shoulder (Plate v. c) [1] ; and ample mantles—(Fig. 4) covering both shoulders, or less commonly, hung diagonally across the back, with a broad turn-back collar (often shaped into points, and sometimes with a cowl behind—Fig. 4, c). In Fig. 4, B, the points of the cloak are tied into knots. Cloaks were worn by exquisites and military men, but, among other classes, were not so commonly used as gowns until about the middle of the sixteenth century.

Slashes.—By "slashing" is meant the decoration of any part of the attire with slits symmetrically disposed, so as to show either the under-garment or a lining of contrasting material. This fashion appears about 1470, increases in vogue and variety up to about 1540, and persists until the middle of the seventeenth century. At first practically confined to the sleeves, from 1500 it rapidly invades the whole apparel, in all sorts of shapes

FIG. 4.—Franco-Flemish. *c.* 1500.

and groupings. In the period under review it is virtually limited to the doublet, the sleeves of which (especially in Italy) are slashed lengthwise and across in various ways, sometimes to such a degree that they have to be fastened together by *points* or lacing, the fine shirting puffing out through the interstices (Plate I. A, B ; and Fig. 3,

---

[1] In Plate v. c, the method of attachment is doubtful, but instances of this use of a cord are found in contemporary illustrations. Fig. 4 (B, C) shows another fastening by means of cords. Presumably in this case they might be pulled tight or relaxed to suit an individual caprice.

PORTRAIT. *F. Ratgerb.*

A, D).[1] Fig. 5 shows a variation of such treatment, the sleeve being laced to the doublet at the shoulder.

OTHER GARMENTS. *Hose.*—These at first correspond to our " tights," but instead of being knitted are made of cloth, silk, or other woven stuff, cut and sewn together. The short doublet reveals them to the waist (Plates I. B ; V. C ; Figs. 2 ; 3, A ; 6 ; 8). Their method of attachment is not always apparent, though the evidence we have, graphic and textual, goes to show that they were laced or tied with *points* (short, tagged laces) to the doublet (Figs. 2 ; 12 ; 14, E).[2] The *codpiece* (a bag - like appendage in front, secured by points or buckles) was universal (Figs. 6, A, C ; 8, A). Striped, embroidered and variegated tights were now in vogue (Plate I. A, C ; Figs. I, B, C ; 2 ; 3, A ; 6 ; 8) ; one leg often differing from the other in colour and design, or the upper portion of the hose being differentiated from the lower. In one variety the part covering the hips rather suggests the " trunks " of the modern acrobat (Fig. 6: see

FIG. 5.—German. *c.* 1500.

note [1] below). The slashing and puffing of hose belongs more properly to the next period. A kind of over-stocking turned over at the top about the knee is a common fashion in Western Europe during the last

---

[1] Fig. 6 shows a form of decoration which is superficially like slashing, but here the process is different. Instead of the structure of the garment being cut into slashes, bands of another material are added (*appliqués*).

[2] At this period many pictures of men engaged in strenuous physical effort and partially stripped for action—headsmen, wood-cutters, etc.—show the hose worn with points untrussed for greater freedom. We venture to suggest that, generally, the attachment of the points was deliberately concealed ; in which case they were perhaps affixed either to the inside of the doublet or to the waistcoat (inner doublet: see note, p. 5).

decade of the fifteenth century (Fig. 1, A, B). It may be an early form of boot-hose (see Chapter III.). Apart from this fashion, and excepting also some haphazard arrangements of clothing among the lower classes, it would appear that " hose " proper consisted of a single garment reaching from waist to toe, *i.e.* breeches and stockings combined.

HEAD-GEAR.—Hats and caps were low and moderately flat. The " wide-awake " or petasus type was only worn by rustics, huntsmen, travellers, etc. (Fig. 5). The prin-

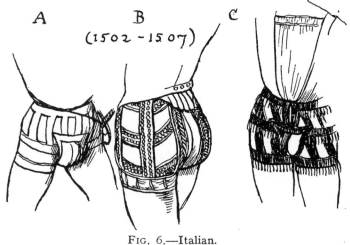

FIG. 6.—Italian.

cipal types are (1) a small round cap with or without a turn-up (Plate I. ; Plate II. A, C, D, E, F ; Fig. 1, A, C; Fig. 7), the crown sometimes pinched or gathered into four lobes, and forming the prototype both of the priestly biretta and of the modern " mortar-board " : (2) a low hat with a broad, platter-shaped brim (Plate I. D ; Plate II. B ; Fig. 2), often decorated with plumes, plain or spangled [1]; soon after 1500 this type of hat tends to become flatter in the crown, and to have its brim variously slittered in tabs, which were doubled over, slashed and

[1] The extravagant proportions to which these plumes sometimes attained are shown in various illuminated MSS., notably the *Roman de la Rose* (British Museum : Harl. 4425).

arranged in a variety of patterns : (3) a flat cap with upturned brim, or flaps, of the playing-card type (Plate V. A, B, C ; Fig. 3, A, B, C). Types (2) and (3) and their variants may have a tie of ribbon or cord to secure them to the head or to sling them behind the shoulder (Plate VI. G ; Fig. 3, A, B), and are also worn over a close scull-cap or network caul (Plate III.). It is impossible here to analyse every variation of these head-dresses,[1] but we may remark that the stiffened brims were frequently decorated with brooches, jewelled badges, or ornamental *points* which also served to loop them up (Plate V.).

FIG. 7.—Italian. *c.* 1490.

HAIR.—The hair was worn moderately long, on the lines of what is nowadays called " bobbed " hair, with a deep fringe over the forehead (Plate IV. G, O). Up to about 1500, dandies might deviate from this rule by indulgence in long flowing or curled locks (Plate I. ; Plate II. D ; Plate V. B ; Figs. I and 7) ; and old-fashioned folk, soldiers, and the lower classes inclined to shorter hair dressed on its natural lines, or covered in a caul (Plate III. ; Plate IV. D ; see under HEAD-GEAR). As a rule the face is clean-shaven.

FOOT-GEAR.—Long-pointed toes go out of fashion from the commencement of this period, and broad, duck-billed toes usurp their place (Plate I. A ; Plate III. ; Fig. I, A, B), growing ever squarer ; the shoe at the same time being cut lower and lower till it requires a strap over the instep (Plate IV. B ; Plate V. A. B ; Fig. 3, C). It should be

---

[1] The section devoted to Henry VII.'s reign in D. C. Calthrop's *English Costume* (vol. iii.), and the chapters dealing with approximately the same period in Quicherat's *Costume en France*, illustrate many characteristic types. A glance through Viollet-le-Duc and Enlart (see Bibliography) will also be useful.

observed that neither boots nor shoes have *raised* heels.[1] Tall boots of varying height are worn, generally with the tops folded over to show the coloured linings (Plate I. B ; Plate II. A, B ; Fig. 2). Some of these boots were but roughly shaped to the leg (Plate II. A, B), others cut to fit closely by means of lacing (Plate I. B), ties, or points (Fig. 8), buckles or even buttons (Plate V. C) at sides, back or front. Note how the high boots may have the tops slit behind to facilitate flexion of the knee (Plate II. A ; Fig. 8). Except for hunting, riding, etc., boots went out of fashion towards 1510.

BODY-LINEN.—The shirt begins to be more conspicuous, and as it is more freely displayed its material is often enriched. It may be found finely embroidered at the edges, in gold thread or coloured silks (chiefly black and red). It is cut pretty full, is often closely gathered into narrow bands at wrist and neck (Fig. 3 ; Fig. 6, C), and forms the regular lining to the slashes of the doublet, instead of the puffed linings of coloured silk which developed later.

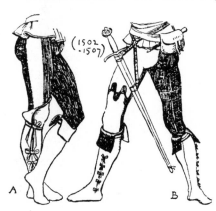

FIG. 8.—Italian.

When the doublet is worn very short, the shirt may be slightly puffed out between the upper and nether garments (Fig. 3, A). The neck is cut low, with an inclination to squareness in front, usually following, when visible, the edges of the doublet and stomacher over back and breast (Fig. 3, A, C) ; but in this, as in most fashions of the period, considerable licence is allowed. When no stomacher is worn, the shirt may appear in front from neck to waist (Fig. 6, C) ; it may also show slightly at the wrists.

ACCESSORIES AND TRIMMINGS.—Linings, facings, collars, and cuffs of costly furs are usual in the outer garments

[1] The first introduction of raised heels will be referred to in Chapter III.

PLATE IV.

FLEMISH. *c.* 1508.

MARRIAGE FEAST AT CANA.

Gerard David.

(particularly gowns) of persons of distinction. Apart from furs the commonest trimmings in this and the next period are broad bands of velvet, embroidery, etc., about the edges. *Points* with beautifully wrought *aglets* (metal tags, often masterpieces of goldsmith's craft) are used all over the apparel as a mere decorative finish (Plate I. B—sleeve). The waist of the outer garment is in most cases confined by a girdle, often highly ornamented, of leather or stuff with metal mounts. The girdle may be slung diagonally over the hips, and supports the pouch and dagger, or the scholar's ink-horn and penner. The *dagger* is either fixed to the pouch, or directly to the belt. There is another variety of girdle, narrow and sash-like, and knotted in front. The *sword* (Plate V. C ; Fig. I, C ; Fig. 3, A) is rare, even among the higher ranks, with civil dress. Jewellery increases in vogue : chiefly rings, brooches, collars, pendants, and badges. The cane is a mere tallish stick with an unobtrusive knob. Almost all metal work is massive in design. *Gloves* (rarely actually worn, but usually carried by persons of rank) are often finely embroidered : the cuff, of different colour or material, is quite short, with tabbed and looped edges, the knuckles slashed, revealing the finger rings. Soft gauntlet gloves are also in use (Fig. 18).[1] The pouch or *escarcelle* (there are no pockets) is commonly a sumptuous piece of work (Fig. 3, C).

WOMEN

BODY GARMENTS.—Amplitude and length characterise the ladies' habits of this age. Gowns were low-necked, the *décolletage* square, rounded, or V-shaped. A variant is open to the waist before (less often behind, Fig. 9, D), the opening, V- or U-shaped, laced across over either a low stomacher or, perhaps, an under-robe. Sometimes the front of the gown turns back in a broad shoulder-collar. Long ample trains are general, spreading from a close-fitting body ; or from a fuller garment, fitting loosely and forming a mass of great folds from the shoulders to the

[1] The gloves in Plate I. are of a special kind associated with falconry.

ground. It is quite usual to find the latter type worn over the former. Both might be made to lace or fasten up the back, and the fuller garment was pretty generally slit down to the waist behind, where, in the absence of a girdle, were affixed points or a brooch by which the train might be caught up out of the dust.[1] Otherwise it was lifted with the hand (Fig. 9, c), or tucked under the elbow (Fig. 9, E). Very broad fur, velvet, or embroidered borders were in vogue (Plate IV. K ; Fig. 9, A, B, C ; Fig. 10, B ; Fig. 11). Sleeves were mostly very long and wide, of a monkish type, or swelling to a vaster compass at the mouth ; the linings of fur or contrasting material might be effectively displayed by a turn backwards over the wrist (Plate IV. C, J ; Fig. 9. In Fig. 9, C, the fullness of the sleeve is caught up and twisted round the arm). Full sleeves confined at the wrist also occur, as well as a survival of earlier fashions in a long close sleeve to the knuckles, turning back at the wrist in a broad cuff. Under-sleeves (whether independent articles of attire or attached to an under-gown) emerge from the spreading upper-sleeves. Whether close or full, these always close in at the wrist. Less common in the West than in Germany or Italy were tight-bodied gowns, the close sleeves slashed, slit and laced together, or with slashed elbow and shoulder puffs ; the delicate chemise bulging through the openings (Plate IV. E, where the chemise sleeve is unusually full).

Cloaks.—Ladies of rank occasionally wore long mantles, tied across the breast with long tasselled cords issuant from ornamented brooches or clasps at the cloak's edge (Plate IV. J ; Fig. 10, C).[2] The special habits worn when in mourning included the mantle.

---

[1] Numerous examples of the fashion of wearing the train turned up to show a fur lining, and fastened at the height of the girdle at the back, are to be found in British Museum MSS. *Roman de la Rose* (Harl. 4425), and Royal 16 F.2 (cf. Fairholt, vol. i., and Calthrop) ; and in brasses (*e.g.*, the Marsham brass, 1525, St. John Maddermarket, Norwich). Fig. 23, c, shows the same fashion.

[2] Cf. Brass of Elizabeth Porte, Etwall, Derbyshire : effigy of Elizabeth, wife of Sir Gilbert Stafford (*circa* 1495), Bromsgrove, which, like the figure in Fig. 10, c, from Great Brington, also shows the old-fashioned " sideless " gown : and portrait of Juana la Loca, wife to Philip I. of Castille, by Jacques de Laethem, Brussels.

c. 1500.

Fig. 9.—Franco-Flemish.

19

HEAD-DRESS.—Note the almost complete disappearance of the earlier fifteenth century head-dresses—the " horned," the " heart-shaped," the towering *hennins*, the " butter-fly " veils, etc.   They are now replaced chiefly by nun-like hoods with long side-lappets and ample folds of stuff hanging at the back.   In France and Flanders the tendency is to show the hair in front ; in England it is more usually concealed.[1]   Three main types of hoods may be distinguished :

(i) The Franco-Flemish variety (Plate IV. F, H, L ;

FIG. 10.—A and B, Franco-Flemish ; C, English.

Fig. 9, C ; Fig. 10, A), of which the front edge, lined with bright colour, was either turned back in a broad fold above the head (Plate IV. L), or hollowed in the upper outline to disclose the front hair and the under-cap (Plate IV. F, H).   Broad folds hung over the shoulders, a slit upwards from the lower edge on either side allowing a lappet to fall in front (Plate IV. L ; Fig. 9, C ; Fig. 10, A).   Latterly this lappet might be looped or pinned, or fastened with a

[1] A number of English sepulchral effigies show that the hair, even where virtually hidden by the hood, flows freely down the back, as in Fig. 10, C.

ECCE HOMO.   *J. Mostaert.*

brooch to a point above the ear (Fig. 10, B). This hood was generally set on an under-cap of linen, velvet, or gold tissue, which showed beneath it. This under-cap was evidently stiffened to the shape of the head, and its outline is particularly distinctive. It is often horizontally goffered or quilted (Plate IV. H, L). The front edge, like that of the hood, was frequently embroidered or jewelled ; the whole head-dress being a favourite vehicle for display.

(ii) The " gable "-hood, a *peculiarly* English mode (Fig. 10, C ; Fig. 11), which, with modifications, held its

FIG. 11.—English. *c.* 1490–1505.

own till close up to 1550. It is also called the " kennel," or " pedimental " head-dress, from its characteristic outline. The rigidly angular top was apparently due to wiring or a stiffened foundation. The jewelled frontlet and the broad band of ornament running over the top and down the front lappets are distinctive features ; otherwise it resembles the type just described. Both types have occasionally a projecting under-cap of linen or gauze (Fig. 9, C ; Fig. 11, A) shading the face. Here we may have the prototype of the next form.

(iii) A plain arched hood, mostly of linen, hanging in

full folds behind ; the fronts, reaching the shoulders, turned outwards at the lower corners (Plate IV. C ; Fig. 20). The back fall of drapery could be folded across and pinned up in a number of ways, the effect usually being formal and severe.[1] This hood was in favour with widows and elderly ladies, who, moreover, often added a close-wrapped *wimple* or *gorget* (Fig. II, A), or else a *barbe* (a bib-like drapery of linen hanging in pleats from the chin) to mask the exposed throat and neck.[2] Dark cloth, silk, or other material, as well as linen, might be used for the main construction : in process of time the sides tended to be curtailed and the central dip to be emphasised, till the well-known " Mary Queen of Scots " hood (the French *attifet*) was developed about the middle of the sixteenth century.

A light gauze veil, retaining the peculiar frontal outline of our third type of hood, while revealing most of the hair, is seen in Plate IV. M. Here and in Plate IV. E we approach the more specifically Italian modes. In Italy the hair was very commonly worn uncovered, or covered only at the back by an ornamented net or cap ; from which often descended a long " pig-tail," decorated with ribbons or jewels, or wrapped round with the same material that composed the head-covering.

Cauls, hair-nets, and rich turban-like rolls increase the number of possible varieties of head-dresses. They are more usual in Germany and the south. Exclusively Germanic is a form found in Dürer's prints—a sort of coif surmounted by a high curved transverse crest, beneath which the hair is concealed.[3]

---

[1] For a later instance, see Fig. 55, D.

[2] The barbe is well shown in the brass of Elizabeth Porte already mentioned (note 2, p. 18) and in the well-known crayon portrait by Janet *F*. Clouet of Mary Queen of Scots in mourning for her first husband, Francis II. (the so-called " deuil blanc ").

[3] Examples of the above-mentioned Italian fashions, easily accessible in reproductions, may be found in Ghirlandajo's " Life of the Virgin " (Sta. Maria Novella, Florence, 1486–90) ; " The Legend of St. Ursula," by Carpaccio (Venice, Accademia, 1490–5) ; the frescoes by Pinturicchio in the Piccolomini Library at Siena, 1502–7 ; and in portraits of Bianca Maria Sforza, wife of the Emperor Maximilian. The German head-dress alluded to is seen in Dürer's well-known print, " The Promenade " (Bartsch 94—*c*. 1495), and in his portrait of Felicitas Tucherin (1499: see also Plate IV. A).

HAIR.—The treatment of the hair is so inseparably connected with the *head-dress* that we have already studied the principal fashions in the foregoing sub-section. Additional points to be observed are that with the Franco-Flemish hood and the arched linen hood we find the hair mostly parted in the centre and dressed in flat *bandeaux* at the sides, especially by the younger women (Plate IV. H, L; Fig. 9, C, E; Fig. 10, A, B), a mode also found in England even with the " gable "-hood (Fig. 10, C; Fig. 11, B); and that brides wore their hair flowing loose over their shoulders, with a wreath or diadem round the head (Plate IV. J). This last mode was retained right through the sixteenth century—by country folk even into the seventeenth.

HOSE were long sewn stockings, gartered above the knee.

FOOT-GEAR.—The shoes, seldom visible beneath the full skirts, resemble the men's. Thick-soled *clogs* or *pattens* were sometimes strapped to them.

LINEN, so far as visible, also resembled that of the men. It is often conspicuously displayed by the cut and slashed sleeves (Plate IV. E), and sometimes rises towards the neck to mitigate the effect of the *décolletage* (Plate IV. E, K; Fig. 9, D; Fig. 10, A).

ACCESSORIES. — What has been said of the men is in a general way true of the women. The girdle either resembled the masculine types, the narrow, knotted sash included (Fig. 9, B; Fig. 10, B), or had a long hanging end with an ornamental finial passing through a buckle at the waist (Fig. 23). Note that till about 1525 the waist-line tends to rise. At the girdle hung a pouch, a Book of Hours, or a rosary (Plate IV. C; Fig. 23) — even, sometimes, a dagger. A variety of neck-chains will be observed among the illustrations.

NOTE.—The reader who wishes to extend his acquaintance with contemporary illustrations may refer with advantage to the plates in

Fierens-Gevaert, *Les Primitifs Flamands* ; besides the other material indicated in several foot-notes. The masculine dress of the whole sixteenth century has been classified in its chief details in a series of chronologically arranged outline diagrams by Mlle. de Jonghe, in her articles, " Bijdrage tot de Kennis van de Kleederdracht en de Nederlanden en de XVIe eeuw " (*Oud Holland*, vols. xxxvi.–xxxvii.).

BEHEADING OF ST. JOHN THE BAPTIST.   *Anon*

II

PUFFS AND SLASHES: THE GERMAN ELEMENT
(1510-1545)

SQUARENESS and breadth are the distinctive features of this epoch for both sexes. Full puffs and wholesale slashing invade the male apparel from top to toe. Originating after 1477 among the Swiss, who developed it to extremes and retained it latest, this indiscriminate slashing was enthusiastically taken up in Germany, notably by soldiers (*landsknechte*) and exquisites. Their influence popularised it up to a point in Western countries. We find, however, two checks upon its entire acceptance: the Italianate tradition, lingering into the 'twenties, and from about 1535 the growing influence of Spain. Again, the women are more chary of adopting the foreign element, and retain, throughout, many features of their previous " conventual " modes. Both sexes, till towards 1540, tend to a high-waisted style, especially in the 'twenties. Slashing reached its zenith between 1520 and 1535, its chief luxuriance occurring in the sleeves and the masculine *hose*.

MEN

BODY GARMENTS.—It is, perhaps, even more difficult than before to distinguish the *doublet* from the *jerkin*, as the latter in many cases approximates in closeness of fit, and even in brevity, to the former.

The *doublet* is still generally low-necked,[1] and up to the 'thirties is often found with a deep square *décolletage*. In the course of that decade a gradual rise takes place, till

[1] But see Fig. 12 and Fig. 14, A.

29

about 1540 we have an actual collar; which, thereafter, grows steadily more high-necked. The skirtless form of doublet persists into the 'thirties, but the tendency is to have short skirts, often tabbed or scalloped.[1] The breast may be puffed and slashed. The wrap-over form occurs

1515

FIG. 12.—Flemish.

in either doublet or jerkin (Fig. 14, B). The sleeves for the most part are full, also puffed and slashed, but tight at the wrist.

The *jerkin* remains much as before; though, as has been said, often shorter, and similar in cut to the doublet. It may be sleeveless or with hanging sleeves. Puffed sleeves to the elbow are also not uncommon; these sometimes

[1] These tabbed or scalloped borders are the original *piccadils*.

30

PLATE VII.

ENGLISH. 1528.

SIR THOMAS MORE AND FAMILY.

Holbein.

31

PLATE VIII.

FLEMISH. *c.* 1530.

THE PRODIGAL SON.

Anon.

33

have close continuations to the wrist, or hanging sleeves attached. Lapels and collars are square and pronounced, and the collar is occasionally marked off from the lapel by a "step." The *bases* or skirts of the jerkins, arranged in formal vertical folds (Plate X. ; Plate XI. C, D, H, I), last

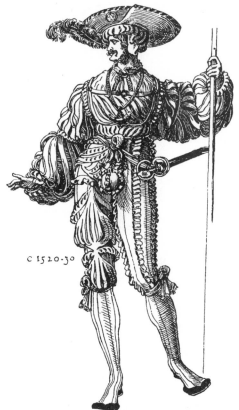

C 1520.30

FIG. 13.—A German *landsknecht.*

throughout this period ; after about 1530 they rarely reach below the knee, and the formal folds tend to go out from about 1540.

Gowns, both long and short (Plate VI. B ; Plate VII. B, C, D ; Plate X. ; Fig. 15), are squarer at the shoulders and more pronounced in outline. The sleeves are as in the jerkin; facings broad and deep "sailor" collars.

Cloaks are rarely worn at this date in the West.

35

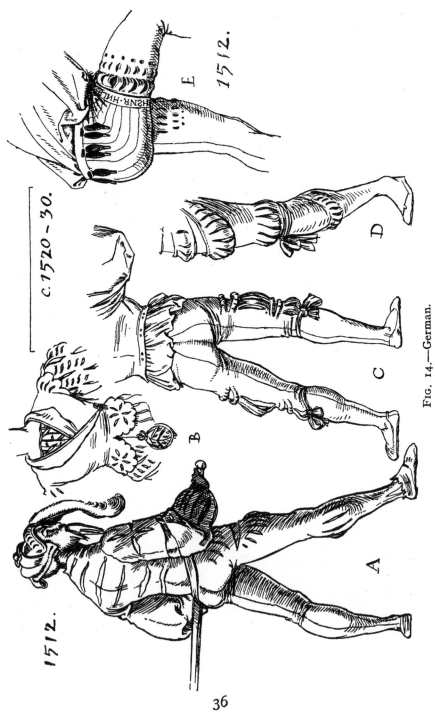

FIG. 14.—German.

PLATE IX

FLEMISH. c. 1535.

J. van Hemessen

C
A "LUPANAR."

B

A

PUFFS & SLASHES : THE GERMAN ELEMENT

The *hose* are now commonly divided into two parts—
the *upper-stock* (or breeches) and the *netherstock* (or stocking).
The two portions are generally permanently united, and
really form a single garment from waist to toe ; but the
breeches are differentiated from the stocking by being
puffed and slashed in the most varied manner, or by means

FIG. 15.—German. *c.* 1540.

of changes in colour, pattern and material. The stocking,
though sometimes striped, is at this date not so often
slashed.[1] In the first half of this period the legs frequently
differ from each other in pattern and colour. *Garters* now

---

[1] The examples in Fig. 14 are rather specially characteristic of extreme German
and Swiss *landsknecht* fashions; but in the sculptures illustrating the Field of the
Cloth of Gold, at the Hôtel du Bourgtheroulde, Rouen, both Henry VIII. and
Francis I. also have the puffing and slashing continued well below the knee.

come into favour: mere ties of ribbon knotted below the knee (see illustrations *passim*).

HEAD-GEAR.—The first type of cap mentioned in the preceding chapter is relegated about the 'twenties to clerics, scholars, professional men, and the unfashionable sort. More fashionable is a low flat bonnet with a *béret*-like crown and a spreading brim slightly upturned or variously looped and tabbed (Fig. 16). The profusion of feathers often found till the 'twenties gives way to a couple of small ostrich tips or to a single plume laid along the brim (Plate VI. C; Plate X.; Fig. 12; Fig. 13; Fig. 14, A). The brim itself, often very wide till about 1530, shrinks after that date, becomes quite plain, and is either flat or slightly drooping. Towards the end of the period the close coifs and under-caps become rare, except for elderly men, lawyers, etc.

1520

FIG. 16.—German.

HAIR. — "Bobbed" hair, moderately long, continues in fashion till the 'thirties, but from the 'twenties short hair grows in favour. Short beards, round or square-cut, come in with the 'twenties; gradually they are worn of greater length, till in the 'forties even young men may wear quite long beards. The moustache follows its natural growth.

FOOT-GEAR.—The toes of the shoes, very square cut, now spread to ludicrous width; the uppers sometimes barely cover the toes. Towards 1540 this width is reduced, and the shoes presently become round-toed, the uppers, rising over the entire instep, being variously slashed or even jewelled. Boots were rarely worn except by huntsmen, travellers, etc. The current fashion is followed in slashing and in the shape of the toes; otherwise the description in Chapter I. holds good.

HENRY VIII.   *School of Holbein.*

LINEN.—The low-necked shirt, embroidered as before, was gathered at the top and wrists into a small frill. From about 1525 it rises up and encircles the throat with a broad neck-band, the opening in front being tied across, in many instances, with small cords or laces, as in Fig. 13. The

FIG. 17.—German.

doublet is often left partly open to show an embroidered front. Small turn-over collars gradually develop, sometimes with a little ruched edge, foreshadowing the Elizabethan ruff (Plate x.).

ACCESSORIES.—*Swords* begin to be worn (especially by the upper classes) with civilian dress. They are generally cross-hilted, but from the 'twenties onward the *knuckle-bow* (the curved bar from cross-guard to pommel) is found in use. The sword-belt, slung obliquely, is often connected with a horizontal girdle. The *dagger*, sometimes suspended by a tasselled cord, is worn as before. Points, gloves, pouches, and jewellery undergo no special change, but there is a leaning towards even greater ostentation in decorative details than in the previous period. *Thumb-rings* are in fashion. The *cane* often has a massively wrought pommel.

WOMEN

BODY GARMENTS are practically unchanged till about 1525. From about 1530 the level front line of the *décolletage*

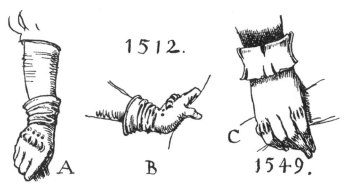

FIG. 18.

tends to arch slightly upwards (Fig. 19). The *corsage* fits closely; and the full skirt gradually loses its train, till finally it just reaches the ground all round. The gown sleeves swell to a wide bell-mouth, and are turned back in a broad fold (often fur-lined) at the elbow (Plate VII. E, H, J; Fig. 19). The undersleeve is either close-fitting to the wrist (Plate VIII.)—with or without slashing—or cut flat and wide, the back seam, curving in to the wrist, left open, and tied across with points, between which puffs out the chemise (Plate VII. E, G, H; Fig. 19). In the latter part of the period the skirt is often open in front in a ∧-shape over the petticoat (Plate XI. B, J), and tends to hang in a funnel form. The open-fronted bodice, laced across, gradually dies out. A novelty is a small shoulder-cape (usually of darker material than the dress), or a close-fitting yoke-like piece, with a standing collar.[1] Towards 1540 we also find high-necked gowns, often with open standing collars (cf. portraits of Catherine Howard, and

FIG. 19.—English.

Holbein's " Princess Christina of Denmark," 1538, in the National Gallery).

HEAD-DRESS.—The three main forms of Chapter I. persist, with modifications, throughout this period, the

[1] Not represented in the illustrations. The type referred to is clearly shown in the well-known series of costume drawings by Holbein in the Basle Museum, and frequently occurs in pictures by Cranach and his school.

tendency being to shorten them at the sides. Occasionally we find close cauls or nets, and flat bonnets after the

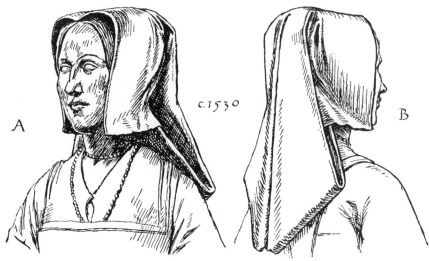

FIG. 20.—German.

FIG. 21.—English.

masculine fashion. These were more popular in Germany, Italy and Spain. The under-cap worn with the " gable "-

hood is sometimes shown in Holbein's drawings with a narrow band fastening under the chin (Plate VII. K, G).

HAIR.—*Where visible*, commonly parted smoothly from the centre. In France, from about 1530, it is often frizzled out on the temples. With the "gable"-hood, the space between the hood and the forehead is generally fitted with two "rolls"[1] or pads overlapping in the centre. These "rolls" appear to have consisted of hair brought forward from the sides and encased in silken swathes (often striped),

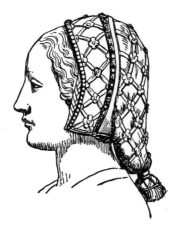

FIG. 22.—French. *c.* 1540-47.

or merely wrapped spirally with ribbon, with the hair showing, as in a Talbot effigy at Bromsgrove, Worcestershire (see also Plate VII. E, F, H ; Fig. 10, C ; Figs. 19 and 21).

BODY-LINEN.—The *chemise*, often richly embroidered, grows high-necked in the latter part of this period. It may have an open, standing collar or a puckered frill at the neck. The wrists close with similar frills. The chemise on occasion opens up the breast.

SHOES.—As under MEN.

ACCESSORIES.—Jewellery grows even more luxurious, pearls in particular being lavishly strewn over the apparel.

[1] Apparently the contemporary term: see Sir T. Eliot, *Dictionarie, s.v.* "Antiae."

The characteristic features referred to in Chapter I. remain.
A sable or marten's skin, the head and claws mounted in

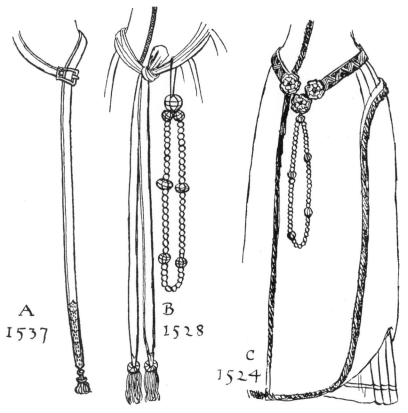

A
1537

B
1528

C
1524

Fig. 23.—English.

gold and jewels, was sometimes hung by a chain from the
girdle and loosely cast about the neck in chilly weather.[1]

NOTES ON THE ILLUSTRATIONS

PLATE VI.—In the figure of the headsman, note the puffing and
slashing of sleeves and thighs, the diagonal breast-slashes caught together
by points, the broad, plumed fur hat slung behind by a ribbon, the
garters of the period, the very low strapped shoes, and the close hair

[1] The pendent marten-skin is shown in the portrait of a woman by Lorenzo
Lotto at Bergamo (Carrara Collection; about 1521—see Berenson, *Lotto*), and in the
portrait of Anna of Bavaria (1556) by Hans Muelich in Vienna, and in Titian's
portrait of the Duchess of Urbino (1537), in the Uffizi.

and square beard. The plumed hat of the lady in the background exemplifies the occasional use of men's fashions by the opposite sex.

PLATE VII.—A good general view of the costume of the English *haute bourgeoisie* about 1528. A and B respectively show the four-lobed ("biretta") and the square ("mortar-board") types of cap previously referred to. Each has at the back a turned-up brim, which in B has a tie over the crown (cf. Fig. 17). The judicial mantle of A is a survival from the middle ages. B has a typical long gown. The full sleeves, slit across at the elbow, are worn diversely : hanging loose on the right but covering the left forearm and hand. C wears the short gown, with puffed elbow sleeves and low standing collar. The ladies show a variety of arrangements of the old "gable"-hood, with the side-pieces—and in E and H the back drapery also—turned up over the crown (cf. Figs. 19 and 21). The much modified hoods in G and K are notable ; among other simplifications the angle at the top gives place to a line curving simply to the crown of the head. In these cases the parted hair is unconcealed in front. In E, F, H, and J the overlapping striped "rolls" mask the hair, and the under-cap reaches below the chin. E, G, and H have the *corsage* open and laced across the front. The wide bell-sleeves, with the huge turn-up at the elbow, show the undersleeves, quilted lengthwise, with the chemise protruding between points at the back.

PLATE IX.—A, B and C are good examples of middle-class "bucks" about 1535. A shows a late specimen of the low-necked skirtless doublet. The codpiece, and the low shoes without fastening over the instep, are clearly seen. A and B wear breeches slashed and puffed from waist to knee (it should be observed that this ornamental treatment does not continue at the back of the leg—see also Fig. 14) : C wears the old long close-fitting hose or tights. In this last figure the sword with knuckle-bow and well-developed guards is of an advanced type. With the exception of A all the men wear the little flat cap so popular later among the London 'prentices. The women's apparel shows little variety, and is essentially plebeian in character. A comparison with analogous figures in other pictures suggests that the arched linen hood and close yoke-like shoulder tippet were in some sort the recognised livery of their trade.

PLATE X.—Points to be noted here are the sleeves of the gown, puffed out to excess on the upper arm and hanging free below the elbow ; the stiffly puckered folds of the skirts of the jerkin ; the white linen puffs "drawn out" through the slashes of the doublet ; the shoes covering the whole instep ; the double sash-girdle ; the attachment of the dagger ; and the little shirt-band with frilled border. It is of course impossible to say whether the hose fit closely, without slashing, to the waist, or whether puffed breeches are concealed under the skirts, between which is seen the slashed codpiece ; but the pattern of the decoration of the codpiece (repeating on the doublet-sleeve) suggests the presence of breeches of like design.

49

PLATE XI.—The fashions throughout are obviously the logical development of those already noticed, and there is little that calls for special
remark. The chief point is the simplification of the breeches which, after
about 1540, rarely cover the knee. Here they form one large slashed
(" paned ") puff on either thigh, with a small rolled and slashed border ;
prefiguring the *trunk-hose* of the second half of the century. The small
collar of dark stuff, falling in two points in front (C, D, G, H, I), is a
novelty and indeed a rarity. The men's head-gear is of the " City flat-
cap " type referred to under Plate IX. C, D, and H show the fluted
skirts to the jerkin, which were out of vogue a little later ; and I shows
plain, unpuckered skirts. The ladies wear a simple form of the French
hood, except M and N, who wear the old-fashioned arched linen hood.

FIG. 12.—The slashing here is very moderate. Note how the short
breeches are definitely separated from the stockings, which here bag over
the garters. Such a fashion at this date was confined to the German
landsknechte and the lower orders. Note also the very marked codpiece,
the plain full sleeves, the *small* plumed cap, the square shoes with ribbon
ties, and the detail sketch of the trussing together of breeches and doublet.

FIG. 13.—An essentially Teutonic personage, and a good example of
the diversity and extravagance of slashing favoured by the *landsknechte*.
The short sword and the cut of moustache and whiskers are peculiar
to the genus. A point that has yet to be explained is how the very
low shoes are kept on without strap or tie. Note the hat-brim made in
two sections, one overlapping the other ; the puffed and slashed under-
cap with ear-flaps ; the sash-like sword-belt ; and the shirt, with ruffled
frill at the neck and with open embroidered front.

FIG. 14.—Each example is again from a Teutonic source. B wears
a doublet, or perhaps a short jerkin, with lapels, and a wrap-over front
fastened by a point on the left side ; the scalloped skirts are interesting.
In C the eyelets along the edge of the doublet may indicate that the
overhanging shirt conceals points on the waistband of the hose, as shown
in E. We may again observe how the slashing is almost entirely confined
to the front of the leg (cf. Plate IX.). E exhibits very clearly the points
by which the breeches were attached to the doublet.

FIG. 15.—A good instance of the short gown, with sleeves puffed
and slashed on the upper arm and continuing as hanging sleeves. The
garment is similar in type to that shown in front view in Plate X. Note
the points on the sleeves ; also the quilted under-cap, and the undersleeves slashed cross-wise.

FIG. 16.—A good type of fashionable bonnet, with looped and slashed
brim. Note the open neck frill.

FIG. 17.—A and B are simply variants of the square cap, with the
brims tied over the crown, as in Plate VII. B. This kind of head-gear
was worn by the staider folk. C is a cap with flaps which could be let

PLATE XI.

FLEMISH. *c.* 1540.

RUMBEEKE CASTLE.

Flemish master.

51

down and fastened under the chin.[1] The standing collar of the gown in
B is noteworthy.

FIG. 18.—C is a typical glove, for men or women of the better classes,
from about 1530–80.

FIG. 19.—Back and front views of a lady's dress, in all respects such
as has been seen in Plate VII. J. The diamond-shaped construction of
the back of the hood is instructive.   In A the edges of this part are
concealed by a drapery fuller than the broad floating tails shown in B.
Note the shoe and the back of the *décolletage*.

FIG. 20.—Back and front views of the plain " arched " hood (as we
have previously classified it : see Chapter I., text, and Plate IV. C),
which fully demonstrate the disposition of the drapery behind, or, at
least, one fashion thereof.

FIG. 21.—See the remarks under HAIR. A and B appear to differ, as
regards the fullness of the back drapery, in the manner observed in
Fig. 19: A of the present figure corresponding to Fig. 19, B, except that
one of the tails is folded stiffly and brought on top of the head.

FIG. 22.—A French hood. A net or reticulated bag, instead of the
usual drapery, covers the back hair. The jewelled *shaffron*, or frontlet,
lies pretty flat to the head. Often its back edge describes a wider arc ;
but the fashion illustrated, like the dressing of the hair, is typically
French.

---

[1] This identical form of cap is shown with the lappets tied under the chin in
Grünewald's " Christ Bearing the Cross," at Cassel. These tied-up flaps seem to
lose favour from *c.* 1530.

III

SPANISH BOMBAST (1545-1620)

THE distinctive characteristics of this period—long wasp-waists, high collars, stuffed-out hips, and a general rigidity of outline, accentuated by buckram, busks, and above all by *bombast* (padding)—find their fullest expression in what we know as "Elizabethan" fashions. These modes, more accurately described by German antiquaries as "Spanish," keep pace with the advance of Spanish power, and die hard in the first quarter of the seventeenth century, when Spanish traditions still cling tenaciously to European courts. Spain, the avowed ally of Catholic interests everywhere, and closely connected with Germany through her rulers, loomed large in European imagination owing to her commanding position and wealth. In dress as in etiquette, the Spanish manner was the "grand manner"; and Western fashions of this date were mainly derived from Spanish models. Italy (except the Two Sicilies, Milan, etc.) preserved some national character: the German Protestants and the Swiss affected to follow native styles: England and France borrowed or adapted details of dress from a great diversity of sources: hardly a nation but seems to have contributed to the general medley: none the less the sign manual of Spain is writ large across this page in the history of costume.

The style may be traced back in Spain to the 'thirties, or perhaps even earlier. By the 'forties its influence is manifest throughout fashionable Europe. Our period may be roughly divided into three sections:

(*a*) 1545–70, when the "bombasted" type is taking shape.

(*b*) 1570–95, when it is fully developed (reaching the extreme of exaggeration by the 'eighties).

(*c*) 1595–1620, when it gradually declines and disappears.

MEN

BODY GARMENTS. — The long-bodied, close-waisted *doublet*, with its contours stiffened by buckram or bombast, becomes by degrees virtually a corset ; busks being used increasingly from the 'eighties. Between 1575–95 the fashion is carried by dandies to absurd excess, and bom-

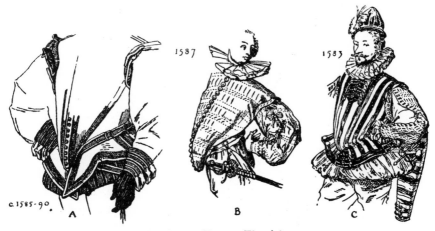

FIG. 24.—Franco-Flemish.

basting reaches its limit in the grotesque *peasecod-belly*, a stuffed-out hump overhanging the girdle in front (Plate XVII. ; Fig. 24, A, B ; Fig. 33, C ; etc.). Till about 1590 the doublet may be often practically skirtless, and in general the skirts are short and the collar is high. Close-fitting sleeves are worn throughout the period, but in the last quarter of the sixteenth century full sleeves of a " bishop " or " leg-of-mutton " cut are affected by the exquisite (Fig. 24, B), and emphasise, by contrast with their breadth, the narrow womanish waist. An intermediate type of sleeve, padded to a moderate fullness and narrowing to a tight wrist, is common in the 'eighties and

'nineties (Fig. 27 ; Fig. 33, A). About the last decade
of our period we meet with sleeves puffed and *paned* from
shoulder to elbow, and close from elbow to wrist (Plate
XXII. A ; and various examples in Chapter IV., of which
Plate XXXI. B will serve as type) ; the breast and back

1611

FIG. 25.—English.

of the doublet being, in such cases, commonly decorated
with long vertical slits. During the whole period the
junction of sleeve and body is usually masked either by
one or more slashed rolls or by a projecting welt known as
a *wing* ; the latter appearing towards the 'eighties. Slashing
keeps its vogue, but is arranged in more formal designs,

the slits being mostly small and not affecting the general outline—except in German-Swiss costume.

The most ordinary type of *jerkin* has the body cut to fit smoothly over the doublet, hence of necessity it is also upon occasion cut on *peasecod* lines (Fig. 24, A, C; Fig. 33, A). When very short-skirted—notably in the 'eighties—

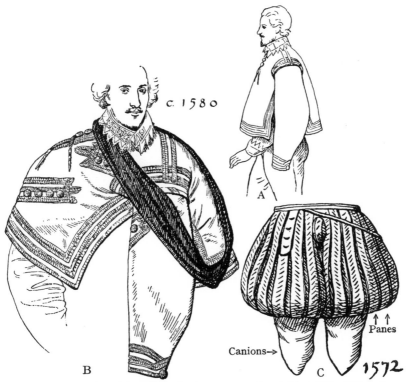

FIG. 26.—A and B, Mandilion (B, from portrait of Sir Philip Sidney); c, trunk-hose with *canions*.

it is often hard to distinguish from the doublet; but there is another clearly marked type, with long full skirts almost hiding the *trunk-hose*. Wings, shoulder-puffs and hanging sleeves are common to jerkin, gown and cloak. The jerkin might be worn closed or open, fastening in front or at the sides. Leather jerkins (buff or *spruce*) were favoured by soldiers and sportsmen, and until about 1575 were often sliced vertically from breast to waist into *panes* (Plate XIII.).

The *mandilion* was a wide jerkin with hanging sleeves. In what is perhaps its most distinctive form (Fig. 26), the body was loose and smock-like, and frequently opened down the sides. It was much worn by soldiers in the sixteenth century, and later became part of the livery of lackeys.

FIG. 27.—Flemish.

FIG. 28.—French. *c.* 1580.

FIG. 29.—French.

Gowns.—In essentials these are as in the preceding period (Fig. 31). Like the cloaks, they often had a standing collar and *facings* (turn-back fronts or lapels), cut, to use a modern term, with a " step." Fur, braid and broad velvet " guards " were their usual trimming. The short variety lingered amongst gallants till about 1570. The sedate long gown now marks the conservative gentry, citizens, officials, scholars and professional men. In the upper classes it is worn by elderly men. It may be worn open, or—less commonly—confined by a narrow knotted girdle.

Cloaks now become very general, with much variety in cut and length. Some scarce cover the buttocks, others reach well-nigh to the feet. Some are collarless, some have falling collars, others again have standing collars and facings. The short *Spanish cape* (Fig. 27; Fig. 33, B) was distinguished by a deep hanging cowl behind in place of a collar.

C. 1580

FIG. 30.—French.

The long French *reître* (Fig. 28) reached nearly to the ankle and not infrequently had a deep shoulder-cape

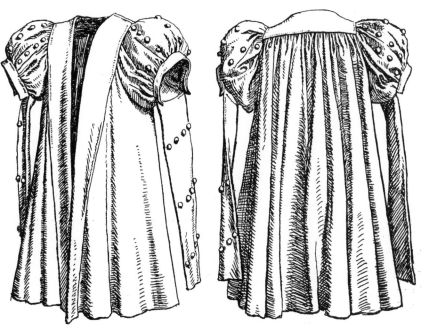

FIG. 31.—German.

(Fig. 30). Hanging sleeves are frequent, and help to cause some confusion in classifying cloaks and gowns. The cloak could be worn in various ways : over both shoulders, or slung from one only, or diagonally across the back (Fig. 29).

BREECHES.—*Trunk-hose* are short puffed-out breeches, often bombasted (with flocks, horsehair, bran, etc.) to

1557

FIG. 32.—Trussing up of hose (Paolo Veronese).

incredible bulk. In cut they are either pumpkin-shaped (Plate XIV.) or gradually spreading from the waist to a broad square base (Plate XIX. ; Fig. 35, A), with every shade of variety between the two extremes. Their average length is to mid-thigh, but the more fantastically fashionable wearers (about 1575–95) often curtailed them to a mere padded roll hardly covering the hips (Fig. 33, B, C).

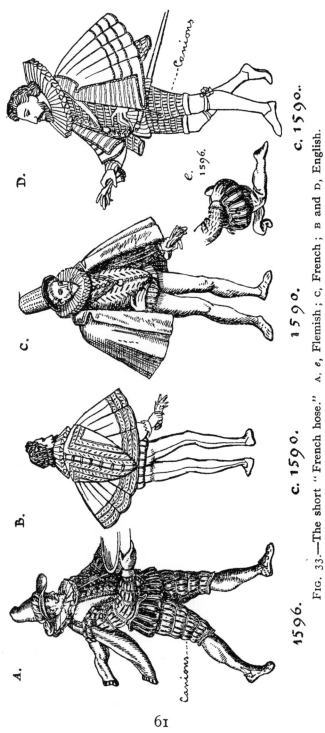

Canions

e.
1596.

D.

C.

B.

A.

c. 1590.

1590.

c. 1590.

1596.

Canions

FIG. 33.—The short "French hose." A, e, Flemish; C, French; B and D, English.

Usually they were *paned*, or cut in vertical bands showing the padded lining between. *Panes* are peculiar to the trunk-hose kind of breeches.[1] After about 1600, the trunk-hose sometimes reach to within a couple of inches from the knee. Plates XII. and XIII. and Fig. 32 show the early form of trunk-hose, with the puffing commencing *from the fork*, not from the waist. Their full development dates from *circa* 1560, and they become an especially dominant feature of sixteenth century dress. " Round hose " and " French hose " are synonyms of trunk-hose.

Venetians are merely what we should call knee-breeches

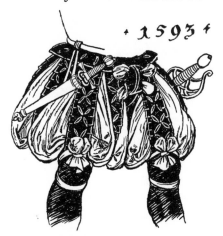

FIG. 34.—Swiss.

Tied or buttoned *below the knee*, their width varies between that of our court-dress and the fullness of modern riding-breeches. Sometimes, too, they are padded. They date from the 'seventies, but are specially in favour in the 'eighties (Plate XV. B ; Plate XVII. ; Fig. 27 ; Fig. 30).

The full slops (like Dutch " knickerbockers ") just reaching the knee, which constitute another type, may be what were known as *galligaskins*.

" Open " breeches, loose, tubular, and unconfined at the knee—resembling in fact our modern " running shorts "—were in vogue *circa* 1585–1610 (Plate XX. ; Fig. 35, B).

[1] Doubtless produced originally by slashing the outer material, *panes* would seem to have sometimes been added bands of stuff sewed down at the ends.

SPANISH BOMBAST (1545–1620)

The *pluderhose* of Protestant Germany are a variant of trunk-hose, having instead of bombast a voluminous limp lining bulging out in huge puffs between the panes (Plate xv. B; Fig. 34).

Canions[1].—These appear *circa* 1570 in conjunction with trunk-hose, which they always accompany except when (as in Fig. 33, B, C and E) the latter are permanently united to the long sewn stockings. They form a kind of tubular continuation to below the knee, and resemble

FIG. 35.—A, Italian; B, Spanish. *c.* 1600.

venetians protruding from under the trunks (Plate XVI. A, B; Plates XVIII. and XIX.; Fig. 26, C; Fig. 28; Fig. 29; Fig. 33, A, D; Fig. 48).

Codpieces (see Chapters I. and II.) begin to go out of vogue from the 'seventies, and practically disappear by the 'nineties. Fig. 34 shows a Swiss survival.

Stockings.—The old tailored stockings hold their own, especially in union with trunk-hose, for a long time; but

[1] See *Burlington Magazine*, vol. xxxii. No. 180, March 1918, "What are 'Canions'?" by F. M. Kelly.

knitted stockings appear early in this epoch, and both kinds regularly become independent articles of apparel, and as such are gartered either inside or over the *canions*, according

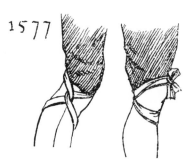

1577

as the last are open or tight at the knee. *Clocks*, of gold, silver, or coloured silk, appear from the 'eighties. *Boot-hose* (for illustrations see Chapter IV.) were a kind of stout over-stocking worn next the boot, professedly to protect the stocking proper. They were nevertheless often of costly materials.

FIG. 36.—Flemish.

The *garter* is often very showy, especially during the latter half of the period, when it may be tied in a bow with deep fringed ends. *Cross-garters* (*vide* Malvolio in *Twelfth Night*) are found as early as about 1525. Their peculiarity is that they are placed below the knee, and the ends, *twisted together cross-wise at the back*, brought forward again and tied in a bow above the knee (Plate XVI. A ; Fig. 34 ; Fig. 36).

HEAD-GEAR.—After about 1565 the flat cap is relegated to the professional classes, to city folk, and elderly men. Among men of fashion it develops into a bonnet with narrow brim (straight or curved), and full, close-gathered crown (Figs. 37 and 39), which grows ever taller till soon after 1590, when such bonnets are discarded.

FIG. 37.—French. *c.* 1555.

This type was in great favour in Spain and Italy.[1] *Hats* are very varied. The brims may be narrow or spreading, straight or curved, or looped up to the crown : the crowns high or low, rounded,

[1] Vecellio terms it *beretta a tozzo*.

square, or peaked.   From the 'seventies broad sombrero
hats appear, which last into the next period.   Another
type, a little toque, worn at the back of the head, either
brimless or with a small rolled brim (sometimes forming a
sort of slashed turban), with a small plume and jewel in

Fig. 38.—French. c. 1555.

front, is fashionable at the French court during the 'eighties
(Fig. 40).   Elderly men sometimes wear cauls tied under
the chin, or skull-caps, beneath their ordinary head-gear.

HAIR AND BEARD.—Close-cropped polls last throughout
this epoch.   From about 1570 to 1590 the gallants generally
wear their hair short behind and bristling upright and

outward like a halo round the face. French courtiers in the 'eighties sometimes dress it in a crop of close curls over

FIG. 39.—French. *c.* 1572.   FIG. 40.—French. *c.* 1585.

the pate, or even, woman-like, in a pair of wired-up arches over the temples.[1] From the 'nineties the hair may be

FIG. 41.—Flemish. (c) *c.* 1595.

worn rather long (Plate XVIII.) ; about 1600, very occasionally, hanging down to the shoulders. The flowing

[1] A fashion mentioned in the *Journal* of Pierre de l'Estoile.

"cavalier" locks are rare till about 1630. The *love-lock* (a single side-lock or plait dangling to the breast, sometimes adorned with ribbon) makes its appearance from about 1600. Pointed beards are the most common. About 1545–55 the beard is often grown long, even by young men, and the fashion is revived towards 1600. In the last quarter of the sixteenth century there is much variety: close beards, forked beards, *spade* beards (square and spreading, of the

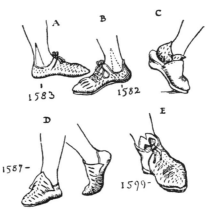

FIG. 42.

"goatee" kind), etc.: shaven chins are exceptional, except among very young men. We read of *starched* and dyed beards; red (vermilion ?) being one freak of fashion.

The moustache, till about 1570, is trained on its natural lines, and later is brushed stiffly upwards. The whiskers often shrink to nothing about 1600.

BODY-LINEN. — Embroidered shirts are still in vogue. The turned-down shirt collar (*band* or *fall*) holds its own throughout the period, though for a time overshadowed by the elaborate *ruff*, which it eventually (*c.* 1630) supplants. There is much variety of construction and size in both. The ruff, at first a mere "ruffle" or tuckered edging to the band, is not formally developed till about 1560. The "sets"

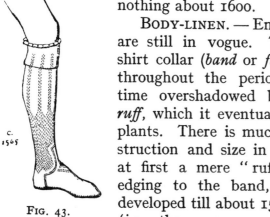

FIG. 43.

(*i.e.*, the arrangement of the pleats) show great diversity after 1580. The huge cartwheel ruff of the 'eighties was starched and supported on wires.[1]

[1] See discussion of *supportasses, rebatos,* and *pickadils,* in "Shakespearian Dress Notes," by F. M. *Kelly, Burlington Magazine,* vol. xxix., Sept. 1916.

Various *coloured* starches are mentioned, but are not apparent in contemporary paintings.[1] After 1610 appears the fan-shaped, wired-out *whisk*, projecting stiffly under the chin (Plate XXI.—the forerunner of the smaller *golilla* in Velazquez portraits, *e.g.* his " Philip IV " in the National Gallery) ; and an informally puckered *falling ruff* was very popular at the close of this period and the beginning of the next (Plate XXII.). The *ruffle* at the wrist accompanies the ruff (though never rivalling its extravagance) ; the turned-back *cuff* is the complement of the band, but is sometimes worn with the ruff. Ruff and band were fastened

FIG. 44.—A, Flemish ; B, English.

in front by strings (Fig. 44, A ; which also shows the fashion of the 'sixties, recurrent occasionally till the end of the period, of leaving the ruff open at the throat). These strings could be left hanging loose or tucked into the collar of the doublet. Low necks are unusual. Lace—including gold and silver lace—now appears, and rapidly increases in favour. From the 'eighties it figures largely in neck and wrist wear.

FOOT-GEAR.—Heels in the modern sense are practically unknown before about 1600. Once adopted they become general ; cut high and straight, and often coloured *red* for courtly wear.

[1] An exception may be found in the portrait of the Marchesa Spinola by Van Dyck in Berlin (Kaiser Friedrich Museum), painted at a date which falls just outside the limits of this chapter. She wears a white ruff, but her cuffs are apparently starched *scarlet*.

The shoe, with (in general) a narrow rounded toe, covers the whole foot. From the 'seventies we find a type with a high front, and narrow side-latchets tied with a little bow over the instep (Plate XVI. B; Fig. 42, A, B). The gap between the front of the shoe and the side-latchets tends to widen after 1600, and the latter become mere ankle-straps (Plate XXII.). At the same time the little ribbon-tie develops into a large bow or a formal *shoe-rose*.[1] After 1600 the toes occasionally show a squarish tendency. The variety of slashing will be understood from the illustrations.

The fashionable boot is cut to mould the leg closely, the tight fit being often assisted by lateral buckles (Fig. 30), by lacing, or by buttons down the small of the leg : or a *pinked* (*i.e.* punctured) design is employed to give a certain elasticity to the leather (Fig. 43). Where these artifices are not made use of, it is possible that the use and dressing of particular leathers may account for the closeness of the fit. The length varies, but even the long boots commonly have the tops turned down in a cup-like fold below the knee. White leather is a favourite material, for shoes as well as boots. In Spain a Λ-shaped strap frequently attaches the boot to the trunk-hose in front. The boot-top is often cut into decorative tabs or scallops.

Pantoffles, or slippers covering only the front of the foot and—for outdoor wear especially—equipped with cork soles thickening from front to back, are often worn over the shoes from about 1570–75 onwards (Plate XVI. A; Fig. 42, C).

ACCESSORIES.—Jewellery is much worn ; pearls being freely sprinkled on the dress of some court gallants. Rings are hung from the strings of ruff or band. Earrings are worn, and a small black string threaded through the ear appears towards 1600, but is more usual later. Ornate collars and neck-chains, with jewelled pendants, continue in use. A rose is occasionally tucked behind the ear by the young dandy (a fashion very rarely illustrated). Paint,

[1] The shoe-rose is *not*, as is often asserted, characteristic of Elizabethan modes, but comes in with the early years of the seventeenth century ; and as the *band*, though for a while overshadowed by the vogue of the *ruff*, outlived its rival, so did the bow-tie survive the *shoe-rose*.

patches, and false hair are not unusual from about 1575. Sword and dagger are general. Their method of carriage will be understood from the illustrations. The long narrow *rapier* with complicated guards is the favourite weapon from now onwards. The English middle classes in the sixteenth century favoured broadsword and *buckler* (a small circular *parrying* shield no bigger than a saucepan-lid). The latter could be slung at the girdle and was wielded at arm's length. Such people of substance as went abroad unarmed were escorted by armed attendants.

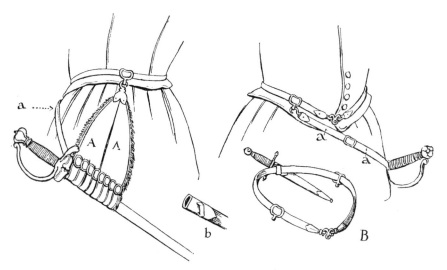

FIG. 45.—Attachment of sword and dagger.

Gloves, till the 'eighties, remain virtually unchanged (Plate xiv. A). The familiar " gauntlet " type, fringed and embroidered, then comes into fashion.

The girdle always follows the line of the waist, so one must conclude that it was often cut on the curve. As often as not it is girt about the doublet under the jerkin, beneath which the *hangers* (Fig. 45, A, A) and side-strap (Fig. 45, *a, a*) peep forth. Masks, covering the face wholly or to the mouth, were worn abroad by both sexes for anonymity's sake, and were sometimes held in place by a button clenched between the teeth.

WOMEN

BODICE.—Bodice and skirt tend increasingly to be separated. In the upper classes, however, the gown in one piece holds its own throughout this period. For con-

FIG. 46.—German.   FIG. 47.—Swiss.

venience' sake we will consider the bodice apart from the skirt. From now on it assumes a definite long-waisted corset form. The waist drops to a pronounced peak in front. The arched *décolletage* of Chapter II. persists till the 'seventies, surmounted by the high-necked chemisette

71

with its frill, or, from 1555, by a formal ruff (Fig. 54, A, B) ;
though the bodice itself is as often high-necked. The
fashion of baring the bosom, re-introduced probably by
Catherine de' Medici in the 'fifties, became again increasingly popular from about 1575. In England at this time

c.1580

A

B

FIG. 48.—French.

it was properly the habit of maidenhood, and as such was
affected by Queen Elizabeth in her latter years. All the
masculine types of sleeve are worn by women. The spreading bell-sleeve, with its huge turn-up elbow cuff (Plates
XXIII. and XXIV. ; cf. Plate VII.) is rare after 1560.
Hanging sleeves are very general. In the 'sixties and

occasionally thereafter till the 'nineties we find exaggerated shoulder-puffs (Plate XXV.; Figs. 47, 48, 49). Loose outer jackets of mannish type (Fig. 46; Fig. 51, A), opened or buttoned, and trimmed with fur and bands of velvet, are worn in cold weather.

SKIRT AND PETTICOAT.—These retain the creaseless funnel form (Plates XXIV. and XXV.). About 1550 appears the Spanish *verdingale* or *farthingale*, a petticoat

FIG. 49.—French.

FIG. 50.—French.

borne out with graduated hoops (Fig. 50*bis*, I*a* and I*b*—the prototype of the " crinoline ") by which this form becomes still more pronounced. The French or " cartwheel " verdingale, which came in in the 'seventies, was a kind of thick hip-bolster (Fig. 50*bis*, II*a* and II*b*) and caused the skirt to spring out to its maximum girth immediately below the waist. In a word, the French verdingale forms a drum, the Spanish a modified cone.[1] The former effect

[1] For a fuller discussion of the *verdingale*, see *Burlington Magazine*, vol. xxix., Dec. 1916, " Shakespearian Dress Notes," by F. M. Kelly. Cf. Sir Roger de Coverley's remarks on his great-grandmother's portrait (*Spectator*, No. 109, 1711).

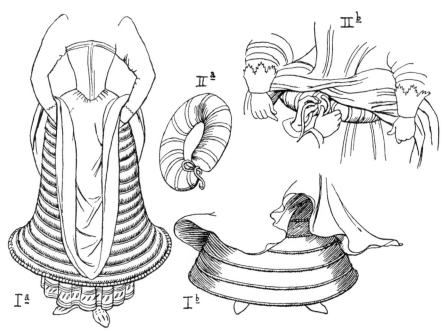

FIG. 50*bis.*—French and Dutch. I, *c.* 1570-80; II, *c.* 1610.

is accentuated from about 1590 by a huge projecting flounce of stuff set in radiating pleats like the ruff, matching the skirt, and resting on the padded hips (Plates XXVIII. B, and XXIX.). The French model, though widely adopted, never quite ousts the Spanish. There are, of course, many intermediate forms. Short (*i.e.* ankle-length) skirts are unusual till about 1610, and go out again about 1620. The overskirt from the

1596.

FIG. 51.—A, German ; B, Venetian.

close of the 'eighties is sometimes worn caught up and tucked under at the sides. The ∧-opening in front occurs throughout the period (Plates XXIV. and XXV.).

HEAD-DRESS.—The *French hood* persists, with slight modifications, until the 'eighties (Fig. 54, B ; Fig. 55, B, C). In England in the 'fifties it often assumes a squarish outline at the top (Plate XXIII.). The arched cap of linen

1609

FIG. 52.—English.

or stuff takes on the curve associated with Mary Queen of Scots (Fig. 55, A ; Fig. 56), and lasts, with trifling modifications, till the end of the period, with or without a pendant veil behind, which is sometimes wired out into arches over the shoulders. From the 'sixties there is a tendency to uncover the hair, even, sometimes, out of doors, with at most a small caul or cap confining the back hair (Figs. 49 and 50) : a fashion which coincides—to the

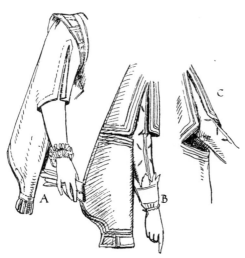

FIG. 53.—Spanish. *c.* 1600–1610.

scandal of contemporary moralists—with the wearing of hats and caps after the masculine patterns, especially for hunting, travelling, etc. (Plates XXVI. and XXVII. A; Fig. 46; Fig. 47; Fig. 54, A; Fig. 57, C).

HAIR. — At the beginning of this period the hair is fluffed out over the temples on either side of the centre parting. In the 'seventies the parting loses favour, the front hair being dressed over wires into a pair of sharply defined arches above the face

FIG. 54.—French. *c.* 1565.

(Fig. 48, A; Fig. 49, B).[1] These develop about 1590 into a high-fronted coiffure trained over pads (Plate XXVII. A; Plate XXVIII., etc.). Contemporaneously is worn a full crop of close curls. False hair is regularly

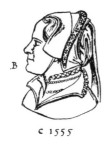

c 1570   c 1555   c 1570   c 1540

FIG. 55.—A, B, C, English; D, German.

employed. Till about 1615 the high broad coiffures over pads remain in fashion (Fig. 57, A, B). In Spain they commonly have a pointed crown. In the second decade of the seventeenth century we already find the bunched-out side clusters of curls and the forehead fringe so popular from about the accession of Charles I. The back-hair during the greater part of the period is most usually dressed in a flat " bun," often confined in a little caul or net. From the 'seventies onward the hair is found generously sprinkled with jewels, especially pearls (Plate XXVII. B; Plate XXIX. B; Fig. 57).

1590.

FIG. 56.—Dutch.

SHOES.—These resemble the men's: in most cases they are hidden by the petticoat. *Pantoffles* and *pattens*, with thick cork soles, are in favour from about 1575 to 1600.

---

[1] The best illustration of this fashion is the well-known Clouet drawing of Marguerite de Valois as a child, in which the course of the wired framework can be distinctly traced. Its French name—*raquette* or *ratepenade*—is given in Henri Estienne's *Dialogues*. See also the alleged " Marie Touchet."

Chopines, with pedestal-like soles, are more specially Venetian, and do not seem to have become popular in the West.

LINEN.—All the masculine varieties of ruff, ruffle, band and cuff are worn by ladies, who had additional forms of their own. Thus till the 'seventies ruff and chemisette are frequently left open in front. As early as the 'fifties, though rarely till *c.* 1575, the latter dwindles and the ruff, wide open in front, and rising like a fan behind the head, edges the *décolletage* (Plate XXIV.; Fig. 48). From the 'eighties we also find a wired-out upright collar of similar fan-like outline as a backing to the *décolletage* (Plate XXIX.;

FIG. 57.—A, B, English; C, Dutch.

Fig. 50; Fig. 57, A, B). This occurs both in plain linen and in lace. From the 'eighties exposed bosoms are pretty general, even with the closed " cartwheel " ruff, and in the last decade of our period the *décolletage* is cut down on occasion below the breasts (Fig. 58). The cuff or turn-back wristband about the same time is often of a deep funnel form, sometimes double, as in Plate XXX.

ACCESSORIES.—Gloves are like the men's (Plate XXIII.). Lace-edged handkerchiefs appear, and little muffs for cold weather. *Fans* are at first of the plumed type shown in Plates XXIV. and XXIX. A, the familiar folding type dating from the 'eighties (Plate XXVII. B). A peculiar stiff fan, shaped like a small flag or vane, seems to have originated in Italy. Hair-dye, paint, and powder (especially after 1610), masks, silken scarves and jewellery of all kinds were made use of. Silk or gauze veils were sometimes (as in the

Fig. 58.—English.

later portraits of Queen Elizabeth [1]) wired into arches above the shoulders. The sable or marten skins referred to in Chapter II. continue to be worn, and small mirrors sometimes hang from the girdle.

NOTES ON THE ILLUSTRATIONS

PLATE XII.—Note the flat cap and plume, the short *gown* with broad facings, long sleeves and puffed shoulders. *Doublet* with low waist, padded ; the neck rather low, with a tiny linen frill. Breeches *paned*, comparatively long and ovoid ; the characteristic swelling commences *from the fork*, not, as later, from the hips (cf. Fig. 32, and contrast with Plates XIV., XVI., etc.). The shoes in this and the next plate are typical *c.* 1545–70. (Frontispiece.)

PLATE XIII.—Observe in this and succeeding plates the very high neck. *Jerkin* of leather with short shoulder-sleeve and double skirt,

[1] *E.g.* the "rainbow" portrait at Hatfield.

the body sliced in panes over the doublet. Skirts, collar, and armholes are cut into "pickadils" (see note on p. 30; "pickadil" is here used in the original sense : a tabbed or scalloped border. In English the word apparently comes into use under James I., *generally* signifying a wired or stiffened under-collar supporting ruff or band—*i.e.* a derivative of the neck-pickadil here shown). Characteristic doublet sleeves and sword with *knuckle-bow*. The gloves and pouch are well illustrated. Breeches as in the preceding instance.

PLATE XIV. A.—The ruff is developing. The *cloak* has hanging sleeves and a standing collar cut with a "step." The short, full-bolstered *trunk-hose* swell directly from the hips.

PLATE XIV. B.—The ruff is developed further. The close sleeveless *jerkin* has a padded paunch. Small pickadils at doublet-wrists. Lace-edging to ruff and ruffles. Most typical *trunk-hose* with obtrusive cod-piece.

PLATE XV. A.—Another sleeveless leather jerkin, worn open in front, with *points* untied : "wrought in Pickendel" (pickadils) at skirt and shoulders, as are the knees of the wide *venetians*. Padded doublet with leg-of-mutton sleeves. Fine ruff and ruffles.

PLATE XV. B.—In purely Teutonic fashion the doublet is relatively short and the waist-line straight. The *pluderhose* (see text of Chapter III.) are in two tiers, and the "pulled-out" lining practically hides the panes. The ties of the *cross-garters* are puffed above the knee. Triple ruff ; conical plumed hat ; horizontal *garnish* of loops across the facings of the cloak ; and clocked stockings.

PLATE XVI. A.—Cloak, with hanging sleeves, slung "toreador" fashion. Short paned trunks with wrinkled *canions* tucked into cross-gartered stockings. A high bonnet is held in the hand, and black *pantoffles* are worn over the shoes.

PLATE XVI. B.—Narrow brimmed high hat with plume : very long pointed waist : trunks with tight, embroidered canions : shoes with side-latchets tied over instep : *falling-band* and *cuffs* of lace : cloak with hanging sleeves.

PLATE XVII.—All the figures wear *peasecod doublets, venetians, ruffs* and *ruffles*—Some diversity exists in the shoes and in the ruffs—most of which are *à la confusion* (*i.e.* with the pleats irregular). Note the full sleeves and the small, close slashing. D has the breeches *pinked*. E has a sleeveless peasecod *jerkin* open over his doublet. The sword *hangers* in C are elucidated in Figs. 24, B, and 45. The breeches of B are buttoned *inside* the knee.

PLATE XVIII.—The trunks are stiffly pleated but not paned : they have close satin canions, over which the stockings are gartered. Small lace *bands* and *cuffs*, the former low at the throat and high at the nape.

SPANISH BOMBAST (1545–1620)

The deep *wings* at the shoulders, and the skirt of tabs overlapping backward, are characteristic from now to the middle of the seventeenth century. The attendant on the right has a broad slouch hat and long riding-cloak or *reître*—"*à la mode de Fraunce.*" Note his ruff baring the throat, and the slashed shoes with side-latchets tied in front. The long hair contrasts with earlier fashions. The three brothers wear " wreathed " cyprus hat-bands (cf. Fig. 41) ; the stylish " servant " is perhaps a kinsman.

PLATE XIX.—Ruff with flattened " sets " : small cuffs : peasecod less pronounced, stiffening to the straighter lines of Plate XXI. : trunks of rigid contour, projecting squarely at the base (cf. Fig. 35, A).

PLATE XX.—Most of the ruffs have flattened " sets," and no ruffles are visible. "Open" breeches are worn, of the kind shown in Fig. 35, B.

PLATE XXI.—Extreme wasp waist, *wings*, skirt of overlapping tabs, and points (possibly mere ornament) along the waist-line : deep lace cuffs and semicircular lace *neck-whisk* (wired out) : very full gathered breeches. Note the long tight-fitting boots, with *heels* and broad spur-leathers ; one boot-top being rolled down and up again below the knee.

PLATE XXII.—It should be pointed out that Dr. van Riemsdijck holds that this work dates from nearer 1630 than the year attributed (1616), and certainly every detail of the costume is found right through the 'twenties. However, we believe that complete corroborative evidence could be found between 1615–20. Note the sombreros, the tied shoes cut away at the sides, and the *falling-ruffs* of most of the men (the remaining two wear laced bands) : also the women's stomachers, their caps with turned-back lace fronts, and the transparent fan-shaped *neck-whisks* (B, C). One man (A) shows the paned upper arm, another the long-skirted buff-coat ; and all have very deep cuffs.

PLATE XXIII.—The whole dress is such as may be found at any time during the 'forties, except the squarish front of the hood, which is characteristically Marian. Note the frills at wrist and throat, and the spreading collar of the upper gown, similarly frilled. The hair is already waved out on the temples (cf. Plates XXIV. and XXV.).

PLATE XXIV.—Sleeves still as in the previous period. Very notable is the wide Spanish *verdingale*. The little jewelled cap with a frontlet like the French hood lasts into the 'eighties. The fan-shaped standing ruff framing the *décolletage* is unusual—except in Italy—before the 'seventies. A feather fan is carried.

PLATE XXV.—Another form of close cap or caul confining the back hair. The front hair is now more definitely arched over the temples. The close sleeves and huge shoulder-puffs are noteworthy.

PLATE XXVI.—The chief points of interest are the high mannish bonnet with plume and jewelled hat-band, and the sleeveless close-waisted open gown, with shoulder-puffs differing from Plate XXV.

EUROPEAN COSTUME AND FASHION

PLATE XXVII. A.—A typically Spanish variety of the high masculine bonnet. The same national character is observable in the set of the lace ruff, close about the chin and ears ; in the shape of the oversleeves, of which later variants are found in Fig. 53 ; and in the *verdingale*, which contrasts with the *French verdingale* in XXVII. B. Note the hair rolled back over a pad, and the close plaited coil behind ; and the row of ornamented points down the front of the skirt.

PLATE XXVII. B.—Open standing ruff ; high jewelled coiffure : leg-of-mutton sleeves, with vast hanging sleeves : jewelled arches of gauze behind the shoulders.

PLATE XXVIII.—Fine coiffures, ruffs, sleeves and *French verdingales*. The hair-dressing of A is repeatedly found in portraits of Gabrielle d'Estrées.

PLATE XXIX. A. — Again the French verdingale, its squareness emphasised by the ruff-like radiating flounce. High standing collar of lace and gauze : hair over pads : deepened *décolletage* : shortened skirt, showing the shoe-roses : plumed cap : deep cuffs : fan, and shoulder-wings. The various ornaments are interesting.

PLATE XXIX. B.—Compare the exaggerated jewelled coiffure with Fig. 57, A, B. The trimming over the crown is apparently of spangled lace. Neck-whisk double, of gauze over lace. The fullness of the skirt is kept rather to the sides, the trimming round the bottom being continued upwards in front almost like a panel.

PLATE XXX.—The hips are but slightly padded, and the deep cuffs are double.

FIG. 24.—Note in A the development of the gloves, the shoulder pickadils and the very short paned trunks. In B and C the doublet sleeves open down the front seam, and are fastened in B with points, in C with buttons. C wears a high bonnet instead of the flat caps in vogue till about 1560–65 ; and his jerkin is trimmed with cords or braids tasselled out at the ends (cf. Fig. 30).

FIG. 25.—An actual suit, worn, according to tradition, in 1611, by an English actor in North Germany. Note the shoulder-wings with slits caught together ; the buttoning of the doublet behind ; the skirt of overlapping tabs ; and the close knee-bands. The doublet is of course also buttoned in front, and the front seam of the sleeve buttons from shoulder to wrist. (From Masner : *Kostümausstellung*).

FIG. 26, A, B.—The typical *mandilion* (see text) : A, as normally worn ; B, "worn to collie-westonward," *i.e.* askew, so that back and front hang over the wearer's arms, while the sleeves dangle fore and aft ; C, paned trunks with *canions* attached.

SPANISH BOMBAST (1545–1620)

FIGS. 27, 28, 29, 30.—Cloaks and other articles of apparel, described under various headings in the text.

FIG. 31.—Short gown of a citizen of Nürnberg. Date, according to M. Maurice Leloir, *c.* 1615. A survival, slightly modified, of an earlier type (Plate XII. ; Fig. 15, etc.).

FIG. 32.—An almost unique illustration of the " trussing " of the hose by means of " points."

FIG. 33.—Contrasts the short trunks having stockings sewn to them (their appearance when doffed is shown in *e*) with such as have *canions* " adjoyned."

FIG. 34.—Compare the attachment of the dagger in other illustrations.

FIG. 40.—This turban-like bonnet is peculiarly characteristic of Henri III. and his *mignons*.

FIG. 41.—Note the rosettes, and the *cyprus* (crape) hat-bands.

FIG. 43.—See text.

FIG. 44.—Note the triple ruff-strings in A.

Fig. 45.—A, A are the *hangers*, carrying the sheathed sword : *a* is the *side-piece* or guide-strap. Both are hooked into buckles sliding on the belt. B, *b*—one method of attaching the dagger to the sword-belt. The dagger sheath is furnished with a staple (like the hasp of a bolt), fixed diagonally. The figure is adapted from a sketch supplied by M. Maurice Leloir. Sometimes the staple is X-shaped, allowing the dagger-sheath to be hung vertically or horizontally. The side-piece (*a, a* in Fig. 45) is at times threaded through the panes of the trunks.

FIGS. 48, A, 49, B, 52 and 54 show the hair wired over the temples *en raquettes* or *ratepenade*. In the first two note the high-puffed shoulders.

FIG. 50.—Typical French court-dress, *c.* 1580–90.

FIG. 50*bis*.—Spanish (I) and French (II) *verdingales*. Sometimes the Spanish has only one hoop—at the hem. The " semi-circled " kind presumably stood out only at the sides and back.

FIG. 52.—Note unusual ruffled edging at top of French verdingale.

FIG. 53.—Spanish hanging sleeves. Contrast Plate XXVII. A, an earlier form.

FIG. 56.—Essentially the same type of cap as Fig. 55, A, but, the side-hair being tucked away instead of fluffed out, the close under-cap is revealed.

FIG. 58.—Obtrusive *décolletage* ; the hair flowing freely down the back generally denotes a bride.

NOTE ON TITLE-VIGNETTE (after T. de Bry, 1592).—The ass-headed dandy is attired " party-wise " in the styles of France (peasecod-belly, *reître* cloak, etc.) and Germany (short-waisted doublet, *pluderhose*, etc.),

83

MAXIMILIAN II.   *A. Mor.*

PLATE XIV.

SPANISH. 1567. B

ARCHDUKE RUDOLF
(afterwards Rudolf II.).

A. S. Coello.

SPANISH. c. 1560. A

ALEXANDER FARNESE.

A. S. Coello.

87

PLATE XV.

A

ENGLISH. 1577.

SIR MARTIN FROBISHER.   *C. Ketel.*

B

GERMAN. 1580.

GERMAN PRINCE.   *Anon.*

PLATE XVI.

A

ENGLISH. 1575.

B

ENGLISH 1583.

SIR JEROME BOWES.   *Anon.*

GEORGE, SON TO *C. Ketel.*
SIR PERCIVAL HART.

PLATE XVII.

D A E B F C

C. Ketel.

CAPT. ROSECRAN'S COMPANY OF BURGHER-GUARDS.

PLATE XVIII.

ENGLISH. 1597.

THE THREE BROTHERS BROWN AND SERVANT.

Isaac Oliver.

EARL OF ESSEX. *M. Gheeraedts.*

PLATE XX.

P. Isaacz.

CAPT. VALCKENIER'S COMPANY OF BURGHER-GUARDS.

99

FRANCIS, EARL OF BEDFORD.   *M. Gheeraedts.*

C

A   B

WEDDING OF D. PLOOS VAN AMSTEL.   *Duyster.*

QUEEN MARY.   A. Mor.

CATHERINE DE MEDICI. *Anon*

PORTRAIT OF A LADY. *Anon.*

(*By kind permission of H.G. the Duke of Devonshire.*)

GRAND DUCHESS JOANNA AND SON. *Anon*

PLATE XXVII.

B

ENGLISH. *c.* 1585–90.

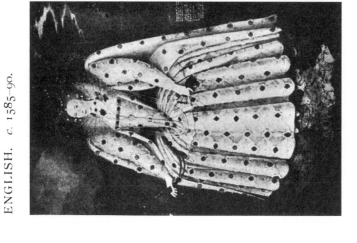

QUEEN ELIZABETH. *M. Gheeraedts.*

A

SPANISH. *c.* 1585.

INFANTA CLARA EUGENIA. *Liaño.*

PLATE XXVIII.

FRENCH. c. 1595.

A

B

C

THREE LORRAINE PRINCESSES.

Flemish School.

PLATE XXIX.

ENGLISH. *c.* 1610.

B. ARABELLA STUART.

M. Gheeraedts.

ENGLISH. *c* 1610.

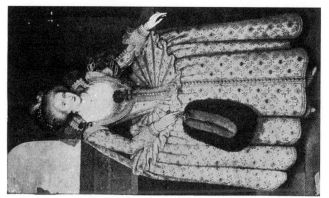

A. QUEEN ANNE OF DENMARK.

M. Gheeraedts.

LADY MARY SIDNEY. *M. Gheeraedts.*

IV

LONG LOCKS, LACE AND LEATHER (1620-1655)

BROADLY speaking, the " Spanish " style falls into disuse from about 1620—at least in modish circles. In the ensuing decade is evolved the picturesque " Cavalier " type of dress, popularly associated with Van Dyck's works, and culminating between 1630–40. Afterwards male attire deteriorates in elegance. The military features introduced with the Thirty Years' War seem to have originated in the Low Countries from about 1600, but the French are the real leaders of fashion from now onward.[1] Old-fashioned folk and staid citizens retain many features of the older dress ; notably the cart-wheel ruff, and the " Mary Stuart " type of woman's cap. The Italians, especially in Naples and Genoa, keep the general " Spanish " fashion till about 1630—Venice holding to a style of her own. The Spaniards create a new national type, as illustrated by Velazquez, Mazo, Murillo, Carreño, and Claudio Coello, which lasts with little change till after 1700.

MEN

BODY GARMENTS.—The doublet throughout the 'twenties retains its busked corset-like body and markedly pointed waist-line, its sloping skirt of overlapping tabs, and the deep shoulder-wings. Though sleeves fitting fairly close occur throughout this period (Plate XXXVII. A, B, C, D, E), the more fashionable type is full and paned to the elbow and close fitting below (Plates XXXI. A, B, XXXII.

[1] Some German authors claim these modes for Germany, forgetting that in Germany itself the exquisite of this date was satirically termed a *monsieur à la mode.*

121

c ; Fig. 59, etc.). The vertical slashing of back and breast (Plates XXXI. B, XXXII. C, XXXV. ; Figs. 59, 61), and the points at the waist (Plate XXXI. A, B ; Plate XXXII. A ; Plate XXXIII. A, C ; Figs. 59 and 61), are fully characteristic of the 'twenties and linger up to the

c 1625.

FIG. 59.—French.

'forties. The changes about 1630–40 are perceptible from the illustrations. Even in the late 'twenties we see a tendency to shorten the waist and lengthen the skirts, and the corset shape is gradually discarded. The skirts are cut more level (Fig. 61, c). The full sleeve—more or less of " bishop " cut—is open down the front seam to the wrist (Plate XXXIII. C; Plate XXXIX.), the opening being often made to button. This type of doublet is commonly left unbuttoned below the breast, giving a glimpse of the shirt (Plate XXXIII. A; Plate XXXV.). The opening, often provided with buttons, from neck to

C 1625-30

FIG. 60.—Italian.

waist down the centre of the back, is a feature found until the doublet is finally (about 1670) superseded by the coat (Plate XXXVIII. F; Fig. 61, C). From about 1640 the doublet is notably shortened, and there is hardly question of waist or skirt (Plate XXXV.; Plate XXXVII. D). The sleeve is sometimes unbuttoned at the wrist and turned up, displaying the lining and the shirt-sleeve more fully (Plate XXXVII. B, D).[1] Towards the close of this period the shirt begins to be visible all round below the shortened doublet (as in the later examples, Fig. 71, A, B).

The jerkin, as a supplementary garment, becomes gradually less common : generally sleeveless or with mere hanging sleeves, it reaches over the hips, and is more or less waistless. Sometimes it laces up the sides as well as in front. The *military* leather jerkin (or *buff-coat*), with very deep skirts spreading and overlapping (Plate XXXIV.

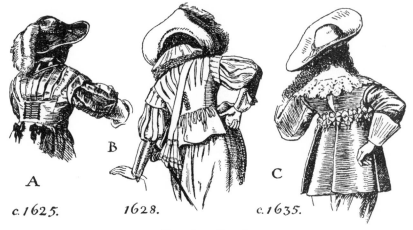

A   B   C

c.1625.   1628.   c.1635.

FIG. 61.—Dutch.

A, E; Fig. 60), is widely adopted. It is generally laced together or tied with points in front, and when without leather sleeves may be provided with sleeves of stuff— in which case a doublet beneath becomes unnecessary (as in XXXIV. A, where no doublet is worn). The sleeves, whether of doublet or jerkin, are in military circles frequently striped or braided round (Plate XXXVII. B). In the 'forties the buff-coat grows short and skirtless (Plate XXXVII. B, F).

---

[1] Hence the coloured lining (of satin, etc.) to the fore-sleeve, still to be found on surviving doublets of 1620–40. An early illustration of this, the prototype of the turned back coat-sleeves in vogue from about 1660 to the end of the eighteenth century, is Frans Hals' " Laughing Cavalier " of 1624 (Wallace Collection).

LONG LOCKS, LACE & LEATHER (1620-1655)

BREECHES.—Trunk-hose, though retained as a livery for pages (Plate XLII. C) till the end of the century, become unfashionable about 1620. Full knickers to the knee (Plate XXXI. A), or just below (Plate XXXI. B), finishing with a row of points, are characteristic of the 'twenties. Between 1625–30 the breeches, narrowing from the waistband to below the knee—more akin to " knee-breeches " in the purely modern sense—are accompanied by garters tied in large bows (Plate XXXII. A, C; Plate XXXV.), or by rosettes in the same position, and are not infrequently buttoned at the sides and left unfastened above the garter to show a puffed linen lining (XXXII. C). Another form, equally common after 1630, is cut moderately close and straight, and is unconfined at the knee (Plate XXXIII. A), where from about 1635 an adornment of points (Plate XXXIV. A, E, F), looped ribbons (Plate XXXVIII. B, C), or bands of lace or braid (Plate XXXVII. B, D), pretty generally occurs. After about 1640 this type of breeches—practically a revival of the older " open " breeches (Plate XX.; Fig. 35, B), which seemingly lost favour about 1610—becomes very fashionable, in ever wider and more tubular cut (Plate XXXVII. B, D, F; Plate XXXVIII. A, B, C; Fig. 65). The breeches are usually buttoned in front (Plate XXXIV. A; Plate XXXVII. B), and the buttons may, or may not, be dissembled in a vertical pleat. The waistband, very high till the middle 'forties, falls about the hips from about 1650.[1] From about 1645 the front, waistband, and knees, and sometimes the outer sides of the thighs, are lavishly garnished with ribbon loops.

STOCKINGS and BOOT-HOSE.—In the *beau monde* silk stockings are worn, to the exclusion of other kinds. Several pairs may be put on in cold weather. Between them and the boots are strong linen *boot-hose* (often edged with lace), whose wide tops generally form a lining to the boot-tops (Plate XXXIII. A; Plate XXXIV. A, D; Plate XXXVIII.

---

[1] It seems that the points often seen at the waist of the doublet (Plates XXXI., XXXII. A; Figs. 59, 61) came to be mainly ornamental, and that the breeches were either hooked to the doublet or secured by the waistband.

125

B, C ; Fig. 66, C). Towards 1650 it is not unusual to find boot-hose worn even with shoes (Plate XXXVIII. F ; Fig. 65). Often they are pierced with eyelet-holes round the edges, so that they can be pulled up and attached to the breeches by points above the knee (Fig. 66, A, B). We find, as a substitute, separate *boot-hose tops*, which only differ in lacking the lower part of ordinary boot-hose.

CLOAKS.—The very short cloak of the previous period becomes rare, and its use implies a degree of affectation

After
M. Maurice
Leloir.

FIG. 62.

in the wearer.[1] Longer cloaks are the rule, either collar-less or with a square falling collar (Plate XXXVIII. A, F). They are slung and draped in various ways : from one or both shoulders, diagonally across the back, in *torero*-fashion, or close wrapped like the modern Spanish *capa* (the right-hand corner being flung across the left shoulder, as in Fig. 63, C) ; or again they may be carried thrown or wrapped loosely over the arm. The *cassock*, a loose great-coat-like garment of varying length, with loose sleeves turned up into a square cuff (Fig. 64), was borrowed, like

[1] For an example, see among Abraham Bosse's fantastic cavaliers of 1629.

other features of dress, from the military. Sleeved *cloaks* are also seemingly depicted in contemporary illustrations, and since both cloak and cassock are worn and draped alike it is frequently difficult to classify an example definitely (as in Fig. 63). M. Maurice Leloir, in the *Bulletin de la Société de l'Histoire du Costume*, has propounded an explanation of the methods of fastening by means of cords sewn inside the collar. According to him these cords might be tied round one shoulder (as in Fig. 62, c); or over both

c 1630.

A.

B.

C.

FIG. 63.—Dutch.

shoulders; or over the left and under the right (Fig. 62, A, B); or round the neck. The ends of the cords are often visible (Fig. 62; Fig. 63, A), but the knotting of them together is concealed by the cloak itself or by the broad falling-band or other form of neck-linen. It is usual to turn back the cloak to display the rich lining, and where the doublet and breeches do not match it is common to find the lining of the cloak matching the doublet and the cloak matching the breeches.[1]

HATS.—Till about 1640 the broad-brimmed *sombrero* type is universal (Plate XXXI. B; Plates XXXIII. and

[1] Cf. Van Dyck's picture of Lords John and Bernard Stuart (Cobham Hall).

XXXIV; Figs. 61, 63, 64), with a moderate crown, the brim often *cocked*—*i.e.* turned up at the side or at the front—and garnished with two or three sweeping ostrich plumes (though the plainer folk dispense with these). Later, the exquisites favour a high tapering crown and a flat, often narrowish brim (Plate XXXV.; Plate XXXVII. D), and the long plumes are in part displaced by loops of ribbon (Plate XXXVIII. E). In general, from about 1645

FIG. 64.—A, Dutch; B, French.

the brims are flatter and the crown higher; though a form appears about 1655 which is not unlike our parsons' " shovel-hats " (cf. Fig. 72).

FOOT-GEAR.—This is *par excellence* the age of the *boot*. The long close-fitting boot (Fig. 60) occurs throughout, but with a tendency for the tops to expand; and simultaneously, from about 1625, the vogue of shorter boots with " bucket " tops sets in (Plate XXXI. B; Fig. 59). According to taste, the tops of all boots might be turned down or folded below the knee in a broad cup (Plate XXXI.

A; Plate XXXIII. A; Plate XXXIV. A, D, E; Fig. 66), the better, presumably, to display the breeches and stockings. From about 1645 the fashionable boot-tops are of extravagant compass (Plate XXXVII. B, D; Plate XXXVIII. B, C). Towards 1630 the upper spur-leathers assume a *quatrefoil* shape (Plate XXXI. A), and thereafter grow to huge dimensions (Plates XXXIII. A; XXXIV. A, D, E; Fig. 66, C; Fig. 67). From about 1645 the toes of boots and shoes taper and lengthen to a square end (Plates XXXVII. and XXXVIII.; Fig. 65). The shoes show no other essential change, except that the large shoe-rose (Plate XXXII.) is gradually replaced by a ribbon-tie, sometimes equally large (Plate XXXV.). Red heels,

FIG. 65.—Dutch. *c.* 1650.

FIG. 66.—A and B, Dutch; C, English.

with corresponding edges to the soles, remain in favour in courtly circles. Boots and spurs do not necessarily denote a rider : with them are often worn clogs or pantoffles (Fig. 66, B, C), which may be permanently affixed to the soles.

BODY-LINEN.—This, with the accompaniment of lace, reaches unexampled importance, the fine linen showing at every opening and the shirt growing fuller in body and sleeves. The semicircular *neck-whisk* (Fig. 60) and the multiple *falling-ruff* (Plate XXXI. A, B ; Plate XXXII. C ; Fig 59 ; Fig. 61, B ; Fig. 63, B) hold their own through the 'twenties, but the *falling-band* of fine linen or lace (or both) gradually gains favour after about 1625 (Plate XXXII. A ; Fig. 64), the lace band being edged with deep scallops. In the 'thirties the *band* spreads till it entirely covers the shoulders (Plate XXXIII. A, C, E ; Plate XXXIV. ; Fig. 61, C). The cuffs keep pace with it, at first of a deep funnel shape, but towards 1645 and onward tending to a limp ruffled form (Plate XXXIV. H ; Plate XXXVIII. C). From about 1640 the band shrinks, until (about 1650) it often becomes quite small and loses its " vandyked " edge (Plates XXXVII., XXXVIII.). The tasselled *band strings* are often visible at the throat (Plate XXXXIV. D ; Plate XXXVIII. B, C). The ruff is adhered to by grave and elderly persons (Plates XXXIII. G ; XXXVII. A, H). With full dress, ruffs or bands are worn *outside* cloak or cassock (Plate XXXV. ; Figs. 63, B ; 64).

HAIR AND BEARD.—From first to last the tendency is for the hair to lengthen, the beard and moustache to dwindle. From about 1630 practically every fashionable man wears hair flowing to the shoulders ; parted over the brow, or (from the 'thirties) cut in a fringe (Plates XXXIII. ; XXXIV. ; XXXVII. B, F, G ; XXXVIII. B). *Lovelocks*, plaited or tied with ribbon (Fig. 63, B) last until the following epoch. The pointed chin-beard of the 'twenties tends in the 'thirties to become a small " imperial," or is altogether eliminated, this last fashion being increasingly notable after about 1640. Middle-aged men retain the chin-beard. Old men, and the professional classes, continue to wear the full beard, and hair more or less short, till the end of the period. The moustache, at first rather full and trained upward, gradually shrinks to a narrow line upon the upper lip; and towards 1655 clean-shaven faces are pretty common among younger men.

ACCESSORIES.—The very broad sash, tied in a great bow behind, is more properly a military fashion and very rare in civilian apparel. Soldiers, however, and the many who affected a military exterior, often wore it over the buff-coat (Fig. 60).[1] The old sword-belt with its *hangers* (cf. Fig. 45) still appears (Plate XXXI.; Plate XXXIV.

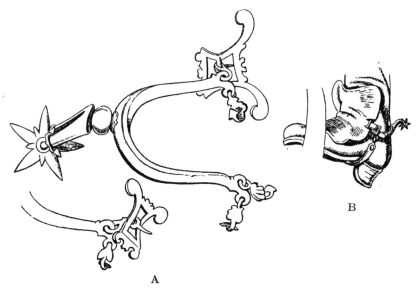

B

A

FIG. 67.—English. A, 1657; B, *c.* 1636.

A), but from about 1625 its functions are increasingly usurped by the *shoulder-belt* or *baldrick*, which was often richly decorated (Figs. 59, 60, and 61, B). The sword is long, with an elaborate guard (see illustrations *passim*); the dagger is now abandoned for ordinary wear. The cane is plain, of convenient walking length (Plate XXXI. A; Plate XXXIII. A). The gloves, of fine leather, are commonly fringed and embroidered and have deep gauntlet-cuffs (Plate XXXI. A, B; Plate XXXV.). Boots are

[1] Soldiers even wore it over the doublet, as in Plate XXXVII., where it is assumed by the wearers *in their character of militiamen*. The steel *gorget* is often worn as well by persons of military pretensions (Fig. 60).

almost invariably accompanied by spurs : these have large rowels and necks bent at an angle, and are set high over the heel (Fig. 67, etc.).

In this, as in the preceding period, to appear in public in *cuerpo*—*i.e.* without a cloak or gown—was accounted " bad form " ; on the other hand the hat was very generally worn indoors down to *c.* 1685.

NOTE.—Puritans, as a class, were distinguished from their neighbours *only* by a certain gravity of attire and avoidance of modish extravagances, such as the ribbons, beribboned " love-locks," etc., and many a prominent Puritan differed not at all from other gentlemen. Cromwell, Ireton, Harrison and Hampden wore what we should account long hair. The close-cropped, prim " Roundhead " of popular fancy was by no means the average type. It was the fanatics of the " Praise-God Barebones " pattern who lent colour to Cavalier satires. Under the Protectorate General Harrison appeared in scarlet smothered in silver lace.

WOMEN

BODICE.—The long wasp-waist and exaggerated stomacher remain in fashion till after 1630, but are generally worn under the gown (*q.v.*). Towards 1630, however, appears a low-necked, high-waisted bodice with square tabbed skirts like those of a doublet (Fig. 68), opening over a round-pointed stomacher which generally matches the bodice (Plate XXXIV. B, C). Above and below the elbow the sleeve forms a full, paned puff, sometimes padded : another form not uncommon before 1630 is the old leg-of-mutton sleeve, fashioned in a series of slashed puffs. A narrow silk girdle or sash, tied with a bow or a rosette in front (or a little to one side), confined the waist, similar decorative fastenings being knotted at the bend of the arm (Plates XXXII., XXXIII. B). The old pointed style of bodice never quite goes out, but rather regains favour about 1650—usually, at this period, without the tabbed skirts or the stomacher (Plates XXXV. and XXXVI.—the bodice in the latter has skirts sloping to a point). Before this, all waists, even when curving downward in front, are high and moderately close. As early as the 'twenties there is a tendency for the sleeves to shrink from the wrists (Plate XXXII.), till by the

'forties they reach not far below the elbow (Plate XXXVI.) ;
and the cuff, from about 1640, ceases, in many cases, to fit
closely to the arm (Plate XXXV.). By the middle of the
'thirties all the old rigidity is banished from the dress, the
sleeve being henceforth gathered in a single large puff,

1639

FIG. 68.—English.

unslashed (Plate XXXVI.), or at most slit up the front
seam. Save for a longer and tighter waist there is sub-
stantially no change after 1650. These later pointed bodices
are generally laced behind—less usually in front, where,
alternatively, they are sometimes clasped with jewels.

SKIRT AND PETTICOAT.—From about 1615 the wheel-
verdingale shrinks in compass, and after the 'twenties it

vanishes (for the time being) from polite society. The skirt is now gathered full about the hips and hangs freely. During the 'twenties it is often tucked up at the sides.[1] Though we find the ∧-shaped opening over the petticoat throughout this period, in the later 'thirties and the 'forties the skirt is more generally closed all round, the open front gradually re-asserting itself after about 1650. Both skirt and petticoat reach the ground.

GOWNS.—Until about 1645 an open gown with close-fitting body and full skirt is regularly worn over the actual bodice and skirt (Plates XXXII., XXXIII., XXXV.). The full sleeves, open in front, end at the elbow, where, till about 1635, they are generally caught together with a bow or rosette, and they are occasionally continued into long hanging sleeves. Very long hanging " dummies " occur in the 'twenties and the early 'thirties.

LINEN, ETC.—Ruffs and the wired fan-shaped collars hold their own till the early 'thirties (Plate XXXII. B, D ; Plate XXXIII. B, D, H) ; in particular elder women and the *bourgeoisie* maintain a preference for the great ruffs ; but towards 1630 the broad falling collar, either high-necked or *décolleté*, grows fashionable and by 1635 is almost universal. The upstanding fan-collar in its last phase is worn in conjunction with the falling collar (Plates XXXII. D ; XXXIII. B, D), which, in its *décolleté* form, opens on the breast in a V, round, or square shape. A kerchief of linen or lace, folded diagonally, is often found after 1635 as an independent upper collar (Plate XXXIV. B, C ; Fig. 70). Towards 1650 the shoulders are bared more and more, till by the close of the period the *décolletage* runs horizontally round the shoulders, sometimes to the entire suppression of visible *lingerie*. The large formal ruffles at the wrist (Plate XXXII.) become *démodé* soon after 1630, being generally replaced by a funnel-shaped, turn-up cuff. The bodice-sleeve is sometimes less formally turned up with lace (Plate XXXVI.), beneath which may on occasion be seen the cuff of the chemise, and a border of linen not

[1] Cf. prints by Callot, St. Igny, Hollar, etc.

infrequently edges the top of the bodice. Richly laced aprons may be worn.

HEAD-GEAR.—Ladies usually go bare-headed, even out-of-doors ; but veils and kerchief-like hoods (either of lace or of dark stuff, and tied with a ribbon at the throat) are worn at discretion. Such hoods come in in the 'forties, and last well into the eighteenth century. Their general aspect is shown in Fig. 86. For riding, hunting, etc., we often see the broad-brimmed masculine hat, with plumes or without. Modified survivals of the old " French hood "

FIG. 69.—Dutch.

and " Mary Queen of Scots " cap, and other lace caps (Plate XXXIII. H), are old-fashioned or distinctly *bourgeois*, and concern principally widows and old ladies.

FOOT-GEAR.—Seldom revealed, the shoes follow the masculine pattern.

HAIR.—The hair is strained back to a flat coil behind, leaving over the brow a varying degree of fringe, and hangs in full bunches of curls over the ears. The tendency is for the side locks to lengthen. The close curly fringe continuing uninterruptedly into the side locks (as in Plate XXXII. B) goes out of fashion, and the close fringe of Fig. 69, A, yields in popularity to a range of carefully separated thin curls (Plate XXXVI.). In the 'forties the fringe is sometimes altogether absent (Fig. 69, B ; Fig. 70), and the side clusters may be more definitely " cork-screwed " (Plate XXXV.) : simultaneously the coil behind grows more conspicuous, and is not infrequently adorned with jewels (Plate XXXV.), ribbons (Plate XXXVI.), or a little projecting caul (Fig. 69, B).

ACCESSORIES. — The indiscriminate extravagance of jewellery which characterises the period from about 1580–

1645

FIG. 70.—Dutch.

1620 now begins to abate. From the 'thirties jewellery is worn rather sparingly, chiefly in the form of chains, bracelets, pendants, earrings, etc. Pearl necklets are in especial favour, and jewelled pendants from the breast-knot (Plates XXXII., XXXIV. B, C ; Figs. 68, 69, B). Pearls also decorate the hair (Plates XXXII. and XXXIV.). Towards 1640 the shortening of the sleeves is followed by the use of long close-fitting gloves (as in Plate XLVI. A, and Fig. 83),[1] generally plain and of fine white or buff leather, confined

[1] Frequently illustrated in prints by Hollar and Le Blond.

about the elbow by knotted ribbons or plaited horsehair *glove-bands*. Their vogue continued till the early nineteenth century, and has since been periodically revived. Muffs are worn in winter. Fans (Plate XXXII. B, D; Fig. 68) were much in use, as were masks for walking abroad or travelling. Patches seem to have come in in the 'forties. The extravagant shapes that figure in pictorial and literary satire do not appear in paintings, where at most we find the small circular spot. Small mirrors are hung from the girdle (Fig. 68).

NOTES ON THE ILLUSTRATIONS

PLATE XXXI.—Contrast the long close boot, turned back and folded under the knee (A), with the short " bucket "-topped kind in B ; and in the latter observe the curious arrangement of buttons on the slashes.

PLATE XXXII.—The cloak of A is the official habit of a *Knight of the Bath*, and must not be confused with ordinary cloaks. In B the peculiar shape of the ruff—its circumference interrupted by a straight section—may be noted as belonging specially to this period, though not of very common occurrence. The *ruffles* in B and D should be distinguished from the *cuffs* in other plates. Those in D are triple, and in the same figure the short sleeve of the gown can be discerned, at the spectator's right, as distinct from the paned bodice-sleeve. In C the panes of the sleeves continue to the wrists, unlike the other examples illustrated.

PLATE XXXIII.—In G and H the retention of former fashions by the seniors contrasts strongly with the more newly fashionable appearance of the younger members of the group. Notice the children's dresses in this and the next plate. It is not easy to distinguish boys from girls.

PLATE XXXIV. is so magnificent a costume picture that every detail merits close study. Observe the hat-plume pared down to a mere fringe of fronds about the crown, as in G : the peculiar braiding of F, which characterises the serving man : the glossy leather of the boots, as in D—it is a common error to suppose that only a suede-like surface was in use at this date : in B and C the short slit oversleeves, with full undersleeves to the wrist : and in D the sleeved under-doublet, of unusual occurrence.

PLATE XXXV.—The sword hung from a waist-belt *under* the doublet should be noticed, also the draping of the cloak and the jewelled hat-band : the more usual hat-band was a mere cord.

PLATE XXXVI.—The extreme simplicity combined with richness of impression is to be remarked. Between 1630–70 plain satins, velvets, etc., unrelieved save for (at most) bands of lace, braid, or embroidery at the edges, are very general.

PLATE XXXVII.—A and D respectively mark the extremes of elderly conservative dress and of youthful fashion. Others of the older men show a leaning towards older fashions. B is essentially military (see note on p. 131).

PLATE XXXVIII.—C represents the *beau* of the period: A, B and F are less dandified. The graceful forms of male attire which came in with the 'thirties have somewhat degenerated. D shows the feminine hood.

FIG. 59.—Note the prevalence of " frogs," or braiding, as a trimming, in this and other illustrations (Figs. 61, A ; 63, B ; 69, A) ; in the last it will be observed that women adopted this fashion, which has already been referred to in a note on Fig. 24.

FIG. 60.—Note the buttoning of the sleeve from shoulder to wrist. The shape of the *neck-whisk* will be better understood by comparison with Plate XXI., which exhibits a stiffer form.

Fig. 61.—Again, in B, the sleeve is buttoned. The sword is frequently worn as here shown, with one-half of the available *hangers* of the baldrick unused.

FIG. 62.—See under *Cloaks*.

FIG. 64.—Note the cassock slit up behind like the modern greatcoat (B) ; and the fastening of the cuffs by means of buttons and loops (A ; cf. Fig. 71, B).

FIG. 66.—A shows points affixed to breeches, for attachment of boot-hose, as in B.

FIG. 69.—B shows an occasional fashion of the side locks, tied with ribbons and hanging to the shoulders after the pattern of the masculine love-locks.

FIG. 70.—Two studies of the same head. The collar, or *gorget*, was often worn double (as in this illustration, where it appears to be merely a square kerchief folded diagonally), or even treble ; and similarly there are instances of a double funnel-shaped cuff (cf. Plate XXX.).

CHARLES I. *Mytens.*

YOUNG CAVALIER. *P. Codde.*

PLATE XXXIII.

A   B   C   D

COUNTESS OF DEVONSHIRE AND CHILDREN.   *Honthorst.*

(By kind permission of H.G. the Duke of Devonshire.)

PLATE XXXIII.

DUTCH 1634.

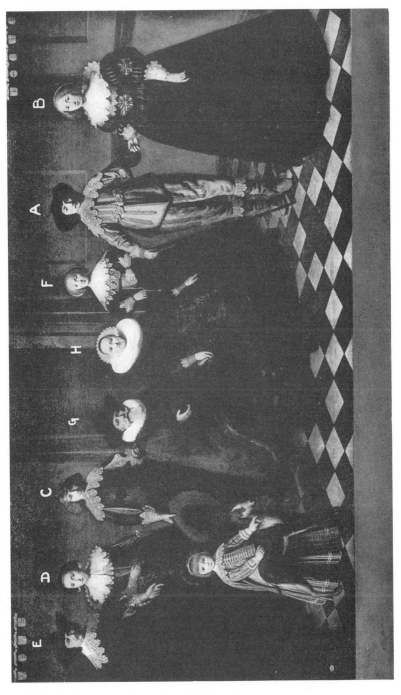

D. Santvoort.

THE JACOBS FAMILY.

PLATE XXXIV.

DUTCH. 1637.

FAMILY GATHERING (DETAIL).

J. M. Molenaer.

147

WILLIAM II OF ORANGE AND BRIDE. A. Van Dyck

PRINCESS MARY.   *Adr. Hanneman.*

PLATE XXXVII.

DUTCH. 1648.

A G B C D H E F

BANQUET OF THE BURGHER-GUARD.

B. van der Helst.

PLATE XXXVIII.

DUTCH. 1652.

DIOGENES.

C. van Everdingen.

V

EFFECTS OF THE "GRAND RÈGNE" (1655-1715)

THE supremacy of France at this date in culture, politics and war makes her the *arbiter elegantiarum* of polite Europe. Among cultured nations Spain alone adheres rigidly to her own fashions and ceremonial.

MEN

BODY GARMENTS.—In its last days the *doublet* is curtailed to a kind of scanty jacket, unbuttoned from the breast and showing the full shirt all round over the breeches (Plate XXXIX.; Plate XL. A, B; Fig. 71, A, B). The short tabbed skirt (Fig. 71, B) is still occasionally seen. Sleeves for the most part reach the elbow, where they are turned up in a close, buttoned cuff (Fig. 71, B), or spread out bell-fashion (Fig. 71, A). Till about 1665 these short sleeves may be made with a buttoned opening down the front (Plate XL. B; Fig. 73). In England, immediately before and after the Restoration, the sleeve appears full, open in front, without conspicuous cuff and reaching half-way down the forearm (as in Plate XXXIX.). A longer form of doublet to the hips, straight and waistless (Fig. 73), or with a close body and full skirt, is sometimes found well into the 'sixties.[1] The doublet disappeared from fashionable circles soon after 1670.

The soldierly *cassock* of the preceding period is now pretty commonly worn as a jerkin over the short doublet (Fig. 72). It is collarless, reaches to the knee, and has full turned-up sleeves.

[1] Cf. Gonzalez Coques' "Family Group" in the National Gallery.

Towards 1670 collarless *coats* and *vests* (or waistcoats) become fashionable, to last, with modifications, till the present day. At first the coat, straight and waistless like the cassock, reaches only to mid-thigh (Fig. 71, c), and the vest not much lower than the waist-line (Fig. 74), but very soon after 1670 the former is prolonged to the knee or just below (Plate XLII. ; Figs. 75, 76), and the vest is gradually

FIG. 71.—Dutch.

lengthened (Plate XLII.) till towards 1680 it is about as long as the coat (Plate XLIV.). There has been some confusion as to the terminology of vests. Evelyn's autograph note on his own copy of *Tyrannus* (Bodleian Library) testifies that a fashion of vests began in England as early as 1663–4. The peculiar costume known as a vest " after the Persian mode," adopted in October 1666 by Charles II. and his court,[1] was an *ephemeral* mode[2] and had little

[1] Diaries of Evelyn and Pepys : Rugge's *Diurnal*.
[2] Evelyn : *Diary*, Oct. 30, 1666 ; Anon. : *Truth of our Times*, 1683 ; Anon.: *Character of a Trimmer*, 1682.

or no lasting influence. It was intended as a counterblast to the craze for French fashions, which after as before retained their supremacy; nor can it be safely identified in contemporary art. The coat-skirts are slit up behind and on either hip: usually these openings are trimmed with buttons (Fig. 71, c; Fig. 75). Until about 1690 the coat is often worn without a vest. After 1675 it is increasingly shaped to the waist (Fig. 76), a character emphasised about the 'nineties by an expansion and stiffening of the skirts (Plates XLV., XLVI.). The full-skirted coat, gathered on either side into a fan-shaped group of pleats radiating from a button on the hip (the origin of the buttons at the back of our modern tail-coats), is carried on into the next period. The buttoned pocket-slits of coat and vest are either vertical (Figs. 73; 74, A) or horizontal (Plate XLIII.; Plate XLVI. E; Figs. 74, B; 76, A, B), and are at first set low. The horizontal fashion gradually prevails over the vertical. Coats are worn indifferently open or buttoned; vests, till the 'nineties, are usually buttoned the whole

c 1650-55

FIG. 72.—Dutch.

way down. From about 1695 we often find the vest buttoned at the waist only, a mode very general by the close of the period. Neither garment has a collar. The coat-sleeves are turned back above or below the elbow in a broad split cuff (Plate XLIII.; Figs. 74, 75, 76), sometimes caught back with buttons. After 1680 the cuff becomes very bulky (Plates XLIV., XLVI.). The vest has similar sleeves which are often turned back *over the coat-cuffs* (Plates XLII., XLV., XLVII. A; Figs. 76, A; 79, A); though these additional cuffs are often dummies, and need not imply the presence of a vest. After 1675 we note a tendency for the sleeve to lengthen towards the wrist (Fig. 76), a fashion almost universal by 1690, though the elbow-sleeve occurs till the end of the century. Latterly the coat-cuff is not invariably split at

the back (Plate XLVI. E; Fig. 79, B). Sometimes, in particular about the 'nineties, a close vest-sleeve to the wrist protrudes from under the coat-cuff (Fig. 79, B). Occasionally a form of coat-sleeve occurs which is not turned back in a cuff, but is slit up the forearm, the slit being arranged to button. This form is found till after the middle of the eighteenth century (see Plate LIII. E). Where the coat-cuff is not uniform with the coat it usually matches the vest.

BREECHES. — The very wide tubular breeches still occur in the early years of this era, but about 1655–70 the favourite mode was the loose *rhinegrave* or *petticoat-breeches*, of which there appear to have been two varieties: (1) a wide kilt (Plate XXXIX.; Fig. 71, A, B); (2) a wide " divided skirt " (Plate XL. A; Fig. 73). They were overladen with ribbons on the lines indicated at the close of the preceding period, and with laces, ruchings, flounces, etc. (Plates XXXIX., XL., XLII., A; Fig. 71, A, B; Fig. 73). The full lining gathered in to the leg frequently hangs from under the outer material (Plate

FIG. 73.—German. *c.* 1663.

160

XL. A ; Fig. 73). Contemporaneously are worn the very full gathered breeches shown in Plate XL. B. With the vogue of the long coat, petticoat-breeches lose favour, though they are not definitely out of fashion till about 1680. Afterwards they formed part of the distinctive livery of " running footmen," in the same way that trunk-hose survived in the costume of pages. Breeches of moderate width gartered at the knee appear in the 'seventies (Fig.

C

1666.

A. c 1670

B. c. 1665

FIG. 74.—Dutch.

71, C) ; another form, *circa* 1675–80, is caught up above the knee in a full gathered flounce[1] ; and in the 'nineties plain close-fitting breeches, fastened at the side of the knee with a buckle or some half-dozen buttons, oust all previous forms. The last are cut full in the seat (fulled on to a waist-band) but otherwise tight ; bare of any trimming, and, when not uniform with the coat, mostly of black velvet.

STOCKINGS, ETC.—Besides the older form of stocking

[1] See the Isham suits in the Victoria and Albert Museum, and Plate LXXIII. A.

we find about 1670–80 long stockings widening markedly from the knee upward. These were often bordered with eyelet-holes and were fixed by points, buttons, etc., over or inside the breeches, sometimes limply "bagging over the garter" (Plate XLIII.). *Boot-hose* or *boot-hose*

FIG. 75.—Franco-English.

tops are still in ordinary wear up to about 1680, and it is not unusual till about 1670 to find two pairs of stockings worn, the inner attached to the breeches, the outer falling back over the garter. A species of drooping vallance of lace, linen, or other material (*cannon* or *port-cannon* [1]) is

---

[1] Not to be confounded with the earlier *canions* (see Chapter III.). For the various late meanings of *canon* in France, *temp.* Louis XIV., see *Notes and Queries*, 2nd series, vol. i., 1916, p. 164.

very commonly affixed below the knee about 1660–70
(Plate XXXIX.; Fig. 73). Garters are below the knee as
before; sometimes, about 1665–80, in the form of a band
trimmed on the outer or both sides with bunches of ribbon
(Plate XL.; Fig. 71, A, C) or gathered falls of lace. All

1684.

FIG. 76, A.—Dutch.

these knee-trimmings go out about 1680–90, when the
stockings begin to be rolled over the breeches, and the
garter becomes a simple buckled band, sometimes hidden
in the rolled top of the stocking (Plates XLVI. and XLVII.).

CLOAKS.—These, except for travelling and the most
practical purposes, cease to be a feature of fashionable dress
after about 1670. Till then the old "cavalier" style

persists (Fig. 74, B), but the tendency is to wear them only in cold or rough weather (Fig. 76, B). They are draped much as we still find them in southern Europe, and continue to be used throughout the eighteenth century, though, from the close of this period, they are generally superseded by loose overcoats.

HEAD-GEAR.—The broad-leaved steeple-crowned hat is

FIG. 76, B.—French. *c.* 1695.

still worn in the 'sixties (Plate XXXIX.), but between 1660–70 the fashionable form is low-crowned, with a moderately wide flat brim [1] (Plate XL.; Fig. 71, A, B; Fig. 72), sometimes " cocked " (turned up), or rolled behind or at the side. From about 1670 very broad brims, variously cocked, are worn (Plate XLII. A; Plate XLIII. A; Figs. 74, 75, 76, A). The

[1] Very similar at times to the modern Spanish *cordovès* as worn by *danseuses* such as Tortajada, and by bull-fighters in mufti.

three-cornered variety comes in about 1690 (Plates XLV., XLVI. E ; Fig. 76, B), and from 1700 is in undisputed supremacy. Ribbons and plumes continue to deck the hat till after 1680 (Plate XL. ; Figs. 71, A ; 74, A ; 75). For the three-cornered hat the flowing plumes are soon discarded in favour of a fringe of ostrich-fronds along

B.
C. 1655.

C.
C 1660.

A .
C. 1675–85.

FIG. 77.—A, French ; B and C, Dutch.

the brim (Plate XLV. ; Plate XLVI. E ; Fig. 76, B). From the 'seventies onward bindings of braid or metal lace become more and more usual (Plate XLIII. A ; Fig. 75). For riding, travelling, or *négligé*, a round cap (*montero*) [1] turned up with fur or stuff is found throughout the period (Fig. 77) ; the flaps could be turned down.

[1] The English form of the Spanish word *montera* (=hunter's cap).

FOOT-GEAR.—Boots, except for riding, went out of fashion soon after 1660. The short " bucket-topped " variety (Fig. 72) vanished. The tall close-fitting boots with tops spreading above the knee continued in use till after 1670, but from about 1665 the rigid tubular *jack-boot* (Fig. 75) was predominant. The lighter forms of jack-boot, from about 1675, were sometimes caught in by buttons or buckles to the small of the leg, and about 1700 high leather leggings or *spatterdashes*, of similar cut, were often sub-stituted, the large square spur-leathers masking the join with the shoe and making it difficult to distinguish in contemporary illustrations between boots and spatter-dashes. From the 'seventies black was the regular colour for men's footwear, though brown leather was used occa-sionally with hunting costume.[1] The boot lost its red heels, which were, however, preserved for *shoes*. These, till about 1680, were worn with round upstanding fronts or tongues. The shoe-rose became obsolete, being replaced by buckles or the old looped tie (Plates XXXIX. and XL. ; Fig. 71, A, C ; the latter often taking the form of a stiffened " butterfly " bow between 1660–80 (Plate XLII. A ; Plate XLIII. A). In the 'sixties small bows of ribbons on the toes also occur (Fig. 73). Finally, from the 'eighties, buckles were the only form of fastening (Plates XLV., XLVI. ; Figs. 76, 80) ; and about this time the front or tongue grew tall and square, sometimes turning over at the top to show the lining (Plate XLIV.). In the 'nineties this turnover was commonly red and cut to a " cupid's bow " curve (Plate XLV. A ; Plate XLVI. C, D, E ; Fig. 80) ; the buckle, at first small and oval, growing larger and rectangular (*ibid.*). The squareness of the toes will be observed throughout the illustrations.

LINEN, ETC.—The shirt, freely displayed by the short doublet of the 'sixties (Plate XXXIX. ; Plate XL. ; Fig. 71, A, B ; Fig. 73), was made very full in body and sleeves. The latter were caught in at the wrist (often with

---

[1] *Buskins* (or close-fitting boots to the calf of the leg) of fine leather or stuff, with turn-over tops and clasps down the front, occur *c.* 1660–90.

ribbon-ties) ; at times also about the elbow (Plate XLIII. A ; Fig. 73). As a rule deep, falling ruffles of lawn or lace trimmed the wrists (Plate XXXIX.; Fig. 71, A ; Fig. 73; Fig. 74 ; etc.). The old *falling-band* or collar, of lawn or lace, was now very deep and oblong (or with rounded corners) over the breast (Plate XXXIX.; Plate XL. A; Plate XLIII. A ; Fig. 71, A ; Fig. 73 ; Fig. 74, B), and so continued till its general disuse towards 1675. From the beginning of the period, or even earlier, we find the *cravat* or neck-cloth,[1] which superseded the falling-band (Plate XL. B ; Plate XLII. A ; Fig. 72 ; Fig. 74, A ; Fig. 75, etc.). This

A. *1689.*   B. *c.1710.*   C. *c.1695.*

FIG. 78.—A, B, French ; C, Dutch.

resembles the misnamed *jabot* of recent feminine fashions. It was tied at first with short spreading ends, usually caught in at the throat with a bow of ribbon (*cravat-string*), or, less commonly, of lace. From the 'eighties the ribbon-tie was generally discarded, and the ends of the cravat, often tasselled, are longer and fall more freely (Plate XLIV. ; Plate XLVI. C, D ; Fig. 76, A ; Fig. 77, A ; Fig. 78, B). The bows of ribbon reappeared between 1690–1700, no longer as a tie but as mere ornament, sometimes double or treble and projecting stiffly from *behind* the falling ends of the cravat (Plate XLV. A ; Fig. 78, A). The long cravat was fashionable well into the eighteenth century. In the early 'nineties

---

[1] In a loosely twisted form the cravat was worn by the military as early as *c.* 1630, though it is rare till after 1640.

appeared the *steinkirk*, with long ends loosely twisted and tucked through a buttonhole of coat or vest (Plate XLVI. E; Fig. 78, C), or else caught into a brooch. Although this fashion became *démodé* before the close of the period, old-fashioned and provincial folk affected it till about 1770. The true *jabot* was a gathered frill of lace or lawn garnishing the breast-opening of the shirt.

COIFFURE.—Periwigs came in about 1660, and by 1665–70 were an indispensable part of fashionable attire.

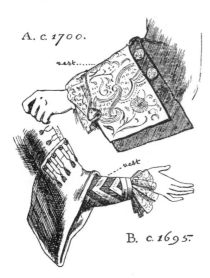

A. c. 1700.

vest

vest

B. c. 1695.

FIG. 79.—French.

The wig was not, as before and nowadays, a careful *camouflage* of natural deficiency, but an avowed substitute for the very long hair which had for some time past been worn. The head, however rich in hair, was regularly cropped or shaven. At first parted smoothly in the centre and hanging in naturalistic curls (Plates XXXIX. and XL.; Fig. 71, A, C; Fig. 73; Fig. 74),[1] the periwig grows more artificial in appearance, and tends from the late 'seventies to degenerate into a ponderous arrangement of formal " corkscrew " curls. It hangs down over breast and back. From about 1690 it rises high over the brow, often in a double peak (Plates XLVI. and XLVII.; Fig. 78). For convenience' sake soldiers, sportsmen and travellers, as early as about 1678, sometimes confined the flowing ends in *ties* at the nape (cf. Chapter VI.).[2] In ordinary civilian circles this fashion did not gain acceptance till after 1710, and then

[1] It is, of course, not always possible in the early years of the periwig to distinguish between it and a natural growth.

[2] A print after Van der Meulen (1678) shows Louis XIV. hunting, with the curls of his periwig gathered back into a tie. Cf. Randal Holme, *Academy of Armoury*, on " campaign " wigs, etc.

only, at first, for "undress." Short but very bushy wigs were often worn for travelling, etc., about 1675–90. Be-ribboned *love-locks* are found till close on 1680. The wig was often exchanged for a nightcap when indoor *négligé* was worn, and the *montero-cap* already referred to was used in the same way on various occasions. Beards were not worn; except, *very occasionally*, a minute tuft on the lower lip. The moustache, after dwindling to a mere thread from the nostrils to the corners of the mouth, vanished after 1685.

ACCESSORIES.—Knots and trimmings of ribbon were lavished over the whole attire in the 'sixties, and continued to be pretty freely worn till about 1680. Afterwards the ribbons survive chiefly in the *shoulder-knot*, which in turn disappears from fashionable wear soon after 1700.[1] This last ornament was worn on the right shoulder (Plate XL. A; Plate XLIII. A; Fig. 71, A; Fig. 73; Fig. 74, A; Fig. 76, A; Fig. 78, A); it was sometimes made of

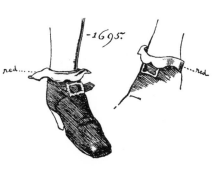

FIG. 80.—French and English.

looped cords, as in the figure in the central background of Plate XLII. The sword-baldrick or *shoulder-belt* grew exceedingly long, broad, and splendid (Plate XL.; Figs. 71, A; 72; 73; 75).[2] A broad loosely knotted sash was often worn about the hips over the coat in the 'sixties and 'seventies (Plate XLII. A): in the 'nineties it was tied formally with short ends hanging level in front, over coat *or vest*. It was often used to confine the shoulder-belt, until that appendage went out of fashion after about 1695; thenceforth the small dress sword, approximating to the present "court" type (Plate XL.; Plate XLII.—against the chair to the right; Figs. 72, 73, 75), was hung from a

[1] It was retained for footmen.
[2] Sword-baldricks quite of this type are still worn on ceremonial occasions by the *suisses* in French churches.

sling or " frog " beneath the vest, and the hilt and sheath peep out from the coat skirts. A broad-ribboned *sword-knot* often decorated the hilt. The sash itself went out soon after 1700. Gloves were mostly plain, and lost the stiffness of their "gauntlets" (Plate XLV. A ; Plate XLVI. E ; Figs. 72 ; 74, B ; 75). Large muffs trimmed with ribbons were worn in winter (Fig. 76, B), commonly slung on a narrow belt or on the sash.[1] The cane, too—preferably a malacca of moderate length—was looped with ribbons, or had a tasselled cord (Plate XLVI. E). Handsome snuff-boxes were carried, and elegant combs, which were ostentatiously used in public by the *beaux*. Paint and patches were affected. Laced and tasselled handkerchiefs (Fig. 77, A) were displayed protruding from the coat-pockets (Figs. 73 ; 74, A ; 76, A).

FIG. 81.—Dutch.

WOMEN

BODICE.—This reverts to its long-pointed, wasp-waisted form (Plate XLI. ; Plate XLII. B ; Plate XLV. B ; Plate XLVI. A ; Figs. 81, 82, etc.), though up to 1670 an intermediate form still appears. It usually has a more or less horizontal *décolletage*, baring the shoulders, and modified, if desired, by the lace border of the chemise, by scarves of lace and gauze variously draped and pinned

---

[1] Examples of this fashion appear as late as 1790. Cf. Plate LI. A, G.

(Plate XLII. B ; Plate XLV. B ; Plate XLVI. A ; Figs. 81, 82, 85, A), or, till about 1690, by a deep falling border or collar of lace hanging straight all round and leaving the neck exposed (Plate XLI.). The bodice was either fastened in front, in which case it was often garnished with bows of ribbon (Fig. 81) or with jewelled

FIG. 82.—Dutch.

clasps ; or was laced behind (Figs. 84, B ; 85, B). In the early part of this period it occasionally has a skirt of splayed-out tabs (Fig. 84). The full puffed sleeve, at first slit up the front (Plate XLI.), reaches to the elbow, or half-way between elbow and shoulder, the shortness of the latter type being compensated by the full sleeve of the chemise (Plate XLII. B ; Fig. 82). Sleeves to the wrist (Fig. 84, c) become old-fashioned after about 1660. The puffed elbow-sleeves were made in close gathers at top and bottom (Figs. 84, 85) ; but from the 'seventies the tendency is to wear wide, straight sleeves, ungathered, and commonly terminating in a fringe of lace or ribbons,

A
1693.

B

FIG. 83.—French:

or a buttoned-up cuff (Fig. 83). In the latter years of our period the elbow-cuff was limp, gathered horizontally and caught at the bend of the arm by a tie or clasp (see Chapter VI.).

SKIRT AND PETTICOAT.—From 1655–75 the skirt is gathered into close pleats about the hips (Plate XLI. ;

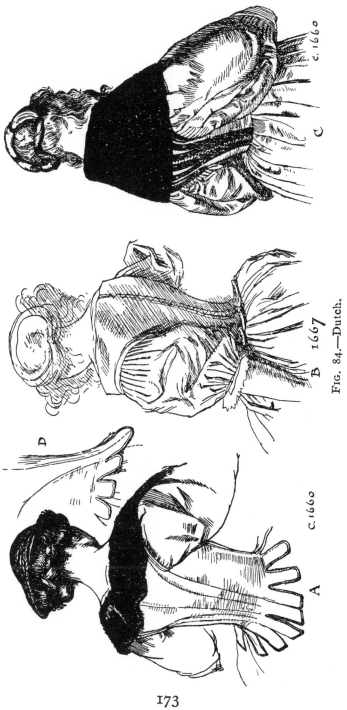

FIG. 84.—Dutch.

Figs. 81, 82). Very commonly it opens down the front over the petticoat, and is looped back to the rear (Plates XLI., XLII. B; Fig. 82), displaying its coloured lining; or else the fronts are caught back at intervals by ribbon-ties or clasps, as in the gown (Plate XLVI. A). The bunching of the skirts behind the hips is marked (see illustrations

b.
1656.

A.
c. 1660.

FIG. 85.—A, Dutch; *b*, English.

passim), and this in the 'eighties is emphasised by regular " bustles " (*culs de Paris*), which immediately after this epoch were ousted by the old *verdingale*—now re-christened *hoop* or *panier*. The petticoat, especially about 1680–1710, was frequently overloaded with ribbons, lace, furbelows and festoons. Both skirt and petticoat trail backwards on the ground.

THE "GRAND RÈGNE" (1655–1715)

GOWNS, ETC.—Gowns, with close bodies not differing greatly in character from the bodice, and with full looped-back skirts and trains, are seen between 1675–1700 (Plate XLVI. A; Fig. 83). Their sleeves follow the current fashions already described. Occasionally loose undress gowns called *manteaux* or *mantuas* are worn. The *sack* is mentioned as early as the 'sixties, but is only recognisable in pictures from about 1715 (see Chapter VI.).

Loose *jackets*, commonly of velvet edged with fur or swansdown, and reaching below the hips, were very often

FIG. 86.—A, French; B and C, Dutch.

worn in the Low Countries about 1650–70 [1]—less often in France or England.

HEAD-GEAR.—Save for loose kerchiefs and hoods (Fig. 86), bare heads remain the rule till after 1690. For riding and hunting many ladies adopted the masculine hat (sometimes, indeed, not only the hat, but the coat, vest, cravat, sash, and even the mannish peruke and light dress sword). Bunches of ribbon adorned the hair (Fig. 81), developing in the 'eighties into rows of large loops (often backed with

---

[1] The type is represented in "The Love Letter" by Terborch (Munich, Alte Pinacothek), and in many other Dutch pictures.

lace) across the crown ; and in these, towards 1690, originated the *fontange, commode,* or *tower.* Each of these names
is applied to the close caps of lawn or lace covering the
back of the head, and rising in front in several tall, wired,
and goffered tiers, which increased in height from front to
back, and projected obliquely forward (Plate XLV. B ;
Fig. 83, A ; Fig. 87). The cap of the commode was generally
trimmed with ribbons, and with long lappets behind, which
could be pinned up to the crown (Fig. 87, B, C, D). This
head-dress held its own, more or less, to the end of the

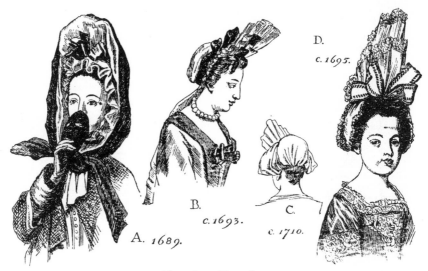

FIG. 87.—French.

period, but reached its climax towards 1700, after which
it tended to dwindle. Kerchiefs and hoods might be worn
over it (Fig. 87, A). About 1710 a little lace or linen
cap, without the special features of the commode, was
fashionable, and soon became the merest apology for a
head-covering (Chapter VI.).

HAIR.—Plate XLI. and Fig. 81 show the characteristic
fashion of the 'sixties, with wired-out side-curls hanging
clear of the cheeks. In the 'seventies these corkscrew
curls hang closer to the face, or, increasingly, are brought
from the nape to hang in front of the shoulders. In the

PROSPECT OF DANZIG (DETAIL).   A   B   *A. Steck.*

A   B

PORTRAIT-GROUP.   *F. Duchâtel.*

GERTRUDE VAN DUBBELDE. *B. van der Helst.*

PLATE XLII.

DUTCH. c. 1670.

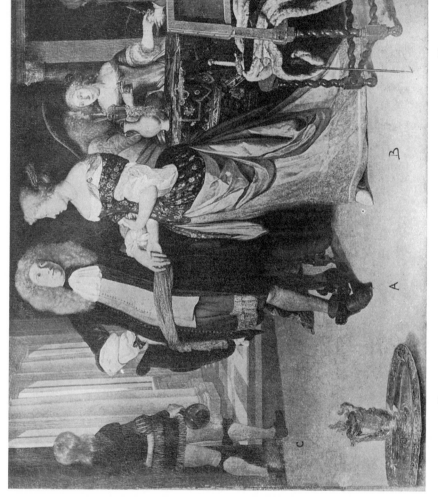

CONVERSATION PIECE.

E. van der Neer.

183

coiffure hurluberlu, a French innovation of 1671, the hair was cut fairly short and closely curled all over the head. Plate XLII. shows the hair worn in close curls round the forehead. A fashion of this latter kind, worn about 1674, was termed a *taure* or bull-head. In the 'eighties the front hair gains in height and loses in width, till by the 'nineties it is dressed high over the brow, often in twin peaks (Fig. 83, B). This last fashion gradually dies out after 1700, and early in the next period the hair is dressed quite close to the head, the long curls from the nape being retained only for ceremonial attire. From about 1700 powder grows in favour. Pearls continue in vogue (Plate XLI. ; Plate XLII. B ; Fig. 83).

SHOES.—From about 1660 excessively high heels, of what is now known as a " Louis " shape, were worn, and the toes tended more and more to a " needle "-point. Fastened with buckles or ribbons (the bow-tie remains in use, for women, till mid-eighteenth century), the ladies' shoes continued for state occasions to be of satin, brocade, or embroidered material. There are occasional instances of tall *buskins*, of satin or fine leather, being worn for hunting ; and *mules* or slippers appear—high-heeled and covering only the front of the foot.

LINEN.—The deep, high-necked collar is still found at the beginning of the period (Plate XLI.). The characteristic edging of the *décolletage* has already been mentioned. From the 'nineties not a few ladies of fashion adopted the men's *steinkirk*, caught up with a brooch (Fig. 83). The full puffed sleeve, showing below the bodice sleeve, was often caught in by ribbons (Fig. 82). From the 'nineties it was often replaced by deep falls of lace hanging from the sleeve of the bodice ; and lace or linen frills in great variety were worn instead of the old formal cuffs and ruffles.

ACCESSORIES.—*Aprons* become fashionable in the 'nineties (Plate XLV. B) ; sometimes quite short, of lace or silk richly embroidered and edged with gold lace. They did not wholly go out of fashion till the end of the eighteenth

century. The long close elbow-glove of silk or fine leather—
the modern " glacé " or " kid " glove dates from before
1685—is now general (Plate XLVI. A ; Fig. 83 ; see Chapter
IV.). White or pale shades were the most popular. From
about 1690 long lace or silk mittens sometimes take their
place. The muff was generally used in cold weather.
Very broad long *scarves* of rich stuff, with decorated ends,
ruched, scalloped, or *appliqués*, were worn, stole-like, in
the 'nineties, and after. Many ladies carried tall canes, and
richly fringed *parasols* of Chinese pattern in summer. The
latter were often borne over their mistresses' heads by
pages. Paint and patches were more popular than ever.
The passion for ribbon trimmings reached its height about
1670–1700, after which they were more sparingly employed ;
and during the same period the dress is apt to be overladen
with embroideries, fringes, flounces, *appliqués*, and the like.
The taste of the *Régence* banished all such heavy ostentation,
and grace and daintiness replaced the rigid pomp of Louis
XIV.

NOTES ON THE ILLUSTRATIONS

PLATE XXXIX.—Characteristic examples of the masculine modes
which became general in Western Europe towards 1660. The youthful
attendant in the rear affords an interesting contrast, being in *Polish* dress.

PLATE XL.—A shows the short sleeve, without a cuff, and trimmed
with ribbon-loops.

PLATE XLI.—Note the looped strings of pearls above the ears, in
place of the more usual bows of ribbon. The lace collar exposes less
of the neck than is usual at this date.

PLATE XLII.—The old trunk-hose are seen (C) in a modified form
as part of the livery of a page. A typical sword and baldrick are displayed in the foreground.

PLATE XLIII.—Note (A) the spreading stocking-tops (Fr. *canons de
bas*), gartered below the knee and caught up over the breeches, presumably by points or buttons ; and the double gather of the shirt-sleeve
The corners of the split coat-cuff, when rounded as in this illustration,
were known as *hound's ears*.

PLATE XLIV.—No ruffles are worn at the wrists (cf. Fig. 71, B), and
no buttons at the fronts of coat and vest. The natural hair is worn ;

an exception, not altogether isolated, to the general wearing of periwigs mentioned under COIFFURE.

PLATE XLV.—The wide coat skirts of A approximate to the style of the next period. He wears the ribbon of the Garter. The shoe has been re-drawn, for clearness, in Fig. 80. In B the hanging sleeve (the original "leading-string" associated with early childhood) is the only detail which differs from adult costume.

PLATE XLVI.—The heavy overlapping pocket flaps of E are characteristic of the latter part of the period. The pocket-slit of D is still vertical.

PLATE XLVII.—The wigs are characteristic of the close of the period, and are *powdered*. B wears what appears to be a horseman's cloak in lieu of dressing-gown. In C the jauntier cut of the coat announces the approaching 'twenties. The servant still wears a form of *fontange* (cf. Fig. 87, c).

FIG. 72.—Note the doublet-cuff turned back over the already turned-up sleeve of the cassock.

FIG. 73.—A German exaggeration of French modes about 1660–70. The doublet has vertical pocket-slits.

FIG. 74.—A shows the tasselled handkerchief in the vertical coat-pocket (cf. Figs. 73, 76). B wears a cloak, coat and vest. C shows the wrist-band and sleeve-links.

FIG. 76.—A is dressed as a sportsman, with a powder-flask slung over his shoulder. B has a heavy tasselled sword-knot.

FIG. 77.—In A we see the usual *négligé*—a dressing-gown over the vest, a montero-cap worn without the periwig, and slippers ; b and c are slightly varying forms of the montero. Sometimes under similar conditions the vest is worn without coat or gown.

FIG. 78, A.—The bows of ribbon projecting behind the cravat, as in Plate XLV. A, are purely ornamental.

FIG. 82.—The plaited lock from behind the ear recalls the earlier *love-lock* (Chapter IV.). Very characteristic of the 'seventies is the swathing of the trimming about the shoulders in a series of shallow festoons (cf. Plate XLII. B).

FIG. 83, A.—The deep puckered flounce or *falbala* of the skirt recurs in Plate XLVI. A. It is very general in the 'nineties. Note the patches, the long gloves, the steinkirk, the tabbed stomacher girdled by a buckled ribbon, and the broad turned-back edging of the body of the gown (cf. Fig. 87, B).

FIG. 84.—In A and C the high-necked velvet pelerine and boa-like fur are worth noting (cf. the little cape in Fig. 86, B). In B the characteristic stiffening of the *décolletage*, exposing the shoulders, is clearly shown.

The sleeve is put in low down (cf. Figs. 81, 85, B). Sleeves of the kind worn by C reach to within two or three inches of the wrist. D is a front view of a corsage similar to A.

FIG. 86.—C is the same type of hood as B, but seen from an angle (not quite in profile) which explains the construction at the back.

FIG. 87.—Note the mask and patch, and the tiny muff at the wrist (A).

MUSICAL PARTY.   *P. van Slingelandt.*

MALE PORTRAIT. *J. Weenix.*

A   B

"OLD PRETENDER" AND SISTER.   *Largillière.*

PLATE XLVI.

FRENCH. *c.* 1710.

A   B   C   D   E   *Largillière.*

LOUIS XIV. AND FAMILY.

195

PLATE XLVII.

FRENCH. c. 1715.

CRÉBILLON AND FRIENDS.

R. Levrac Tournières.

VI

PANIERS, POWDER AND QUEUE (1715-1790)

THE supremacy of French fashions is still almost absolute throughout civilised Europe, even Spanish court circles falling in with the general trend. Towards 1770 English modes assert themselves, even in Paris, especially among men ; but not for ceremonial occasions. We may broadly distinguish the mannered daintiness of the *rococo* period, 1715-60 ; and the gradual decline, 1760-90.

MEN

COIFFURE.—This, as the special characteristic of the age, may for once come first. The old *full-bottomed* wig (Plate XLVIII. C ; Plate XLIX. ; Plate LI. G ; Fig. 93) continues in use till towards the middle of the century, but the fullness tends to be carried to the back, and the long front lappets are rare after *c.* 1730 ; modifications of it (Plate LIII. D ; Fig. 89, A, B ; Fig. 92, D) appear even as late as the Revolution. But from about 1730 it tends to become old-fashioned, and is appropriated mainly to elderly and professional men. In fashionable circles the wig is worn dressed off the face from temple to temple in a low toupet, and tied in a *queue* at the nape. The principal forms of queue are :

(i) The *tie*—a mere bunch of curls caught together by a black bow (Fig. 92, A).

(ii) The square black *bag* enclosing the back hair, and tightened with a draw-string (Plate L. B ; Plate LII. D ; Fig. 88 ; Fig. 94, B ; Fig. 96, A ; Fig. 99, C).

(iii) The plaited *ramillie* (Plate LII. E). Sometimes there are two or even three plaits. Towards 1790 the plaited queue is occasionally looped up and held by a comb at the back of the wig.

(iv) The *pigtail*, tightly encased in a spirally wound

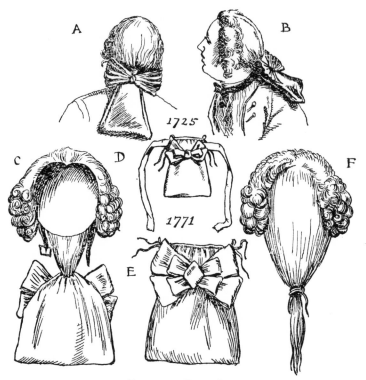

FIG. 88.—Bag-wigs.

black ribbon (Plate LI. A ; Fig. 90, C—a double pigtail ; Fig. 91 ; Fig. 92, B ; Fig. 100, E).[1]

The *catogan* or *club* appears about 1770, and was much in favour with the *Maccaronies*. Its construction is made clear in Fig. 90, A, B ; Fig. 100, B, C ; and Fig. 101, B, C. Full-bottomed wigs, complete or modified, are not worn with tied or plaited queues or pigtails, but usually with the hanging locks and knots shown in our illustrations. In

[1] In Scene VI. (the gaming-house) of Hogarth's " Rake's Progress," the black pigtail-case lies detached from the wig on the floor beside the hero.

Fig. 89, A, B, and Fig. 93, the twisted central *neck-lock* is a survival of the late seventeenth century *dildo*.[1]

The toupet, from about 1750, grows higher and more formal—especially so in the 'seventies (Fig. 92, A), when

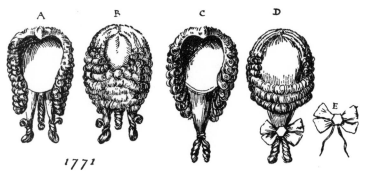

1771

FIG. 89.—A and B, *Perruque à nœuds*; C and D, Brigadier-wig.

the *Maccaronies* carried it to excess (Fig. 96, A; Fig. 100, B). *Pigeon's wings* (bunches of hair bushed out or irregularly curled over either ear) most generally accompany the toupet (Plate L.; Plate LI., A, B, J; Figs. 88,

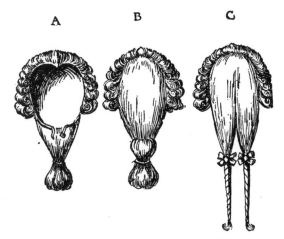

FIG. 90.—A and B, Catogan; C, Double Pigtail. 1771.

94, 95, 102) till about 1740. Later they are increasingly replaced by one or more horizontal roll curls at each side (Plate LIII., A, E; Fig. 91; Fig. 92, A, D; Fig. 101,

[1] See Randal Holme, *op. cit.*, note 2, p. 168.

B, C ; etc.). From the 'eighties a single broad curl often runs from ear to ear above the queue (Fig. 99, C), and from

1778

FIG. 91.—Pigtail.

about the same time dates a broad dishevelled crop (*à la hérisson*) covering the whole head (Fig. 92, B, C ; Fig. 98).

A   B   C   D

C. 1775.   c 1785.   1785.   1790.

FIG. 92.—Wigs, various.

Under the wig the head was shaven or close-cropped, except for an occasional fringe in front or at the nape ;

the former powdered, pomatumed and dressed into the toupet, the latter similarly combined with the queue.[1] Those who preferred their own hair powdered and dressed it to imitate a fashionable peruke. Powder was sometimes omitted, a fashion pretty common for everyday wear after about 1760.

THE COAT.—The distinctive features of 1700–15 become more pronounced, but otherwise, for full dress, there is no essential change till about 1750–60 (Plate XLVIII. C ; Plates XLIX.–LIV. ; Figs. 93, 94, 102). Between 1720–50 the wide skirts are often buck- ramed out to a lamp-shade outline, as if to rival the ladies' *hoops* (Plate LI. A, G ; Plate LII. E ; Fig. 95). Gener- ally the fashionable coat reaches just below the knee, though very occasionally eccentric or ultra-fashionable persons varied the length and modified the closeness of the waist and the width of the skirts in an affectation of rustic styles, which, appearing among the " quality " in

FIG. 93.—French. 1721.

England as early as 1731, were revived at intervals during the century. The coat was worn open, or buttoned at the waist only. In the 'fifties a general shrinkage takes place. The buckramed skirts lose favour, the fronts tend to be sloped away below the waist, and the pleats and hip-buttons shift backwards (Plate LIII. A, E ; Plate LIV. A). From 1760 these changes become more marked. About 1780, for ordinary wear, appears a high-waisted, double-breasted " cut-away " coat (Fig. 98) with pointed lapels. This coat when buttoned disclosed the short vest. It is most strikingly

[1] Luke Sullivan's portrait of David Garrick in the National Portrait Gallery shows the head cropped except at the nape.

developed in the subsequent *Incroyable* or *Directoire* style.

The great split turn-up cuff holds its own into the 'fifties (illustrations *passim*). Plate LIII. A, exhibits a transition to the more moderate type which follows ; here,

FIG. 94.—French.

too, the ruffle alone peeps out from under the cuff, whereas the older cuff commonly falls a trifle short of the wrist, the better to display the full shirt-sleeve (contrast with Plate XLVI. C; Plates XLIX., LIV.; Figs. 93–95 ; and compare the later illustrations). Gradually the cuffs become small and tight, being latterly often a mere border of stuff matching the *collar* (Fig. 99, A ; Fig. 100, B ; etc.). We begin to meet with flat turn-back collars from the late 'thirties, especially with fur-trimmed winter coats. They become more and more general, and, growing broader

1745

about 1780, begin to assume the appearance of a standing collar with a deep turn-over—a type which is fully characteristic of the late 'eighties, and increases in height in the ensuing period (Figs. 92, C ; 98 ; 101, B, C ; 103). The great pocket-flaps dwindle from the 'fifties.

For travelling and country wear various kinds of overcoats are worn, generally loose and rather shapeless, with large cuffs and a flat collar. Overcoats with double and treble capes appear from the middle of the century (Fig. 97 ; Fig. 99, B).

THE WAISTCOAT (originally VEST).—This, in general, till the 'fifties, reaches within an inch or two of the knee

FIG. 96.—English. *c.* 1770.

(Plate XLVIII. C ; Plate XLIX. ; Plate LIII. D, E ; Plate LIV. C ; Figs. 93 ; 94, B ; 95). Shorter waistcoats are seldom seen till later—unless with the shortened coat. Like the coat, the waistcoat often (*circa* 1720–50) had its skirts buckramed in front (Plate L. B ; Plate LI. B ; Fig. 95). At this time the back *skirts* of the waistcoat (*i.e.*

from the waist downward) usually match the front. From the 'fifties the stiffening falls into disuse, and the skirts shrink steadily till, with the 'eighties, appear square-cut, double-breasted, skirtless waistcoats,[1] whose large, pointed lapels overlie those of the coat (Figs. 98, 103). By the more

1780.

1794.

FIG. 97.—French.　　　FIG. 98.—Dutch.

fervent devotees of fashion the long waistcoat is habitually buttoned at the waist only, the *jabot* or frilled shirt-front being displayed in the opening (Plate XLVIII. C; Plate L. F, G; Plate LIV. C; Fig. 95); or, occasionally, a button or two may be fastened at the throat as well, the *jabot* appearing in the unbuttoned interval between throat

[1] Long-skirted waistcoats with curved double-breasted fronts occur much earlier; see Fig. 103, E.

207

and waist ; but with the increasing popularity of the short waistcoat the unbuttoned fashion declines. With the long skirts are worn long sleeves, which often just peep out below the coat-sleeves (Fig. 94, B) ; from the elbow downwards they match the waistcoat-front. Fringed edges to the

FIG. 99.—French.

skirts—survivals from the late seventeenth century—occur until about the middle of the eighteenth century.

BREECHES.—These show little variety. In the early part of the period, in cases where long waistcoats and stockings rolled over the knees are worn, the breeches are hardly visible (Plate XLVIII. C ; Plate LIV. C, etc.). Between 1725–60 they are fairly tight to the thigh, but full and gathered in the seat, and sometimes barely cover the knee-cap. In the latter part of the century they are cut to fit the thighs, so far as may be, without wrinkles. Skin-tight riding buckskins appear from the 'seventies. A buckle and some half-dozen buttons generally secure the breeches at the knee (Plate LIII. A; Fig. 94, B), or for the smoother fit of the rolled stockings they may be without knee-fastenings. From the 'seventies an alternative fastening of bunches of strings or ribbons is found.

FIG. 100.—English.

STOCKINGS.—Often *clocked* with gold or silver for " dress " occasions, till the 'fifties they may be drawn up over the breeches in a flat roll or turn-back fold (Plate XLIX.; Plate LIV. C). The garter (Plate XLIX. A) is generally concealed beneath the rolled top (Plate LIV. C; Fig. 95).

HEAD-GEAR.—The three-cornered hat is retained throughout the period, varying only in its proportions and the relative elevation of the corners. It is as a rule more or less symmetrically cocked till towards 1770: thenceforward the front peak often points markedly upward (*chapeau à la suisse*—Plate LIX. A ; Fig. 99, A, B ; Fig. 101, A), and in the 'eighties we meet with the primitive *bicorne*, the embryo of Napoleon's *petit chapeau* (Fig. 98). The little *Nivernois* hat, beloved of the Maccaronies, is shown in Fig. 100, C, E, F, G.

Wide Quakerish hats were occasionally worn by the plainer sort from about 1700, and with slight modifications became pretty usual for undress from the 'seventies, especially among the sporting fraternity (Plate LXI. A ; Figs. 97 ; 101, C ; 103, A). In the 'eighties appears a hat with a

FIG. 101.—French.

high tapering crown (Plate LXIII.), the precursor of the " top-hat " which followed hard upon it in the next decade.

The *night-cap* (Fig. 100, A, D.) was a customary accompaniment to the *night-gown* (*i.e.* " dressing-gown "), worn for indoor *négligé*, as was the *montero*.

FOOT-GEAR.—Shoes with broad square toes (Chapter V.) still occur throughout the 'twenties, but are superseded by a more normal shape (illustrations *passim*). The tongues or fronts (Plate XLIX. E ; Plate LII. E) dwindle from their previous height and become inconspicuous after the 'forties. Larger, squarer buckles are worn in the 'seventies and 'eighties (Plate LIX. A). For " dress " occasions the red heel endures till the Revolution.

The cumbrous *jack-boot* (Chapter V.) becomes, from

about 1725, the appanage of postilions and their like, and is succeeded by a closer-fitting boot, sometimes shaped to the leg, with a top hollowed out behind the knee and frequently gartered below it with a strap and buckle (Fig. 102). Shaped *spatterdashes* (Chapter V.) of black leather, buttoned or buckled at the side, are also used for

1733.

FIG. 102.—French.

riding. *Top-boots* (Fig. 103) of the sort still worn with little modification by jockeys and huntsmen, appear as early as the 'thirties (see Hogarth, " Rake's Progress "), and become fashionable about 1770. Towards the close of the period they are worn by " bucks," even for walking (Plate LXI. A).

Gaiters, introduced by the infantry about 1710–20, are worn in the country by civilians from about 1770, but are not fashionable till after 1790, having for ages been associated with yokels.

The old-time *boot-hose*, in the form of long white woollen stockings, are occasionally visible above the long riding-boot.

LINEN, ETC.—The fine shirt has a *jabot* (Plates L. G; LII. E; Figs. 91, 95, 96), and ruffles of lawn or lace at

FIG. 103.—English.

the wrist. After the 'twenties *steinkirks*, and cravats with falling ends (Plate XLIX.), are increasingly supplanted by plain folded *stocks* (Plate L. G; Figs. 91, 95), buckled at the nape. A broad black ribbon (*solitaire*) attached to the tie of the wig (Fig. 88, D) often runs loosely about the neck, the ends either disappearing into the *jabot* (Fig. 95; Fig. 96, A, *a*), or caught together by a brooch at the throat.

Till about 1750 we as frequently find it drawn closely about the stock and tied in a bow under the chin (Plate L. B, F ; Plate LI. B, C, J ; Fig. 88, B ; Fig. 94, B ; Fig. 102, A). A new form of cravat, a muslin neckerchief tied in a bow in front, is greatly favoured by the Maccaronies in the 'seventies, and remains in fashion well into the nineteenth century (Fig. 98 ; Fig. 100, C, F ; Fig. 103, A).

CLOAKS of the kind shown in Fig. 76, B, are occasionally worn throughout the period.

ACCESSORIES.—The *sword* ("court" sword or small-sword) was hung from a frog and belt [1] under the waist-coat, or from a cut-steel sling hooked into the waistband. The hilt usually protruded through the skirts of the waist-coat ; when the full-skirted coat was buttoned, the hilt was brought through the side-pleats (Plate XLVIII. C ; Plate LI. B, G ; Plate LII. E ; Fig. 94, B ; Fig. 96, B). Until about the 'seventies it was still pretty generally worn by gentlemen when abroad, but was gradually dis-carded. *Canes* (Plate LI. G ; Plate LXI. D ; Figs. 93, 96, 97, 98, 99) were of varying length, malaccas being the favourite. Amber and ivory knobs, grotesque heads, and tasselled cords were fashionable. Muffs (Plate LII. E) continued to be worn in winter till the end of the period—till 1750, still slung on a close belt (Plate LI. A, G). *Fob-ribbons* with bunches of seals occur from the 'forties, more generally from the 'seventies (Plate LIX. A ; Figs. 96, B ; 98 ; 103, A). Watches were carried in pairs, one being as often as not a *fausse-montre* or dummy. *Snuff-boxes* were more popular and ornate than ever. Laced handkerchiefs, too, were in favour. Many gentlemen affected nosegays. Jewellery was sparingly employed.

NOTE.—The *Maccaroni* plays a conspicuous rôle in English caricature of the early 'seventies (Figs. 96, 100, B, C, E, F, G). The genus was known, but immature, in 1764 : see Walpole's *Letters*. Besides the features already mentioned, he was distinguished by a rather short skimpy coat (Fig. 96) with a flat collar ; a short waistcoat, often without pocket flaps ; a profusion of braiding, tasselled or frogged ; bunches of knee-strings ; large ruffles, and little pumps with buckles, bows, or rosettes.

[1] Clearly shown in Scene II. of Hogarth's "Harlot's Progress."

He was especially partial to striped and spotted stuffs, fobs, and bunches of seals. A tiny *Nivernois* hat surmounting a monstrous *toupet* and *catogan*, a tall tasselled cane and not infrequently a curved hanger (a short cutlass) completed his "make-up."

Care has been taken, in selecting our illustrations of these fashions, to avoid the grosser exaggerations of caricature. Actual portraits of King Christian of Denmark and of his minister Struensee show toupets at least as pronounced as in our figures.

WOMEN

BODICE.—This remained essentially the same : pointed, with a long wasp-waist. The front was either open and laced across (or otherwise fastened) over a stomacher (Fig. 107, D), or closed with false fronts (Fr. *compères*), which were sewn to its inner sides, and commonly laced or trimmed as if an actual stomacher were worn ; or, again, the bodice was uniform, with no indication of a stomacher (Fig. 110, B). A favourite garnish of the bodice was the *échelle*, a series of graduated ribbon bows from bosom to waist (Plate LVI.).[1] The *décolletage* was retained throughout the period, though there was an increasing tendency to mask the bosom with fichus, scarves, etc. (illustrations *passim*). A broad pleat or fold often edged the V opening in front, though this more generally distinguished the "Watteau-backed" *gown* (*vide infra*).

The elbow-sleeve, whether for separate bodice or gown, remained in vogue throughout ; though for ordinary wear the long close sleeve, often on masculine lines, reappeared from the late 'seventies (Plate LIX. C ; Fig. 115, B ; Fig. 116). The short sleeve generally retained its turn-back cuff till about the 'fifties, but from the 'forties gathered or flounced trimmings grew in favour and prevailed over the earlier fashion. The turn-back cuff was very generally caught up by loops and buttons, or other means, into horizontal folds at the bend of the arm (Plate L. E ; Plate LI. D ; Figs. 94, A ; 104 ; 118, B ; 123).

SKIRT AND PETTICOAT.—These, except for ceremonial

[1] Already seen *c.* 1660 (cf. Fig. 81).

wear, were not unusually of ankle length from 1730 onwards. The skirt was generally open in front—gathered
full on the hips and less markedly behind, till in the 'seventies
and 'eighties the taste for lateral extension was more or less
counteracted by the revival of the *bustle* (*q.v.*). The front,

FIG. 104.—English. *c.* 1740.

or the entire circumference, of skirt or petticoat, was often
richly decorated with broad ruches, flounces, etc., variously
disposed. *Trains*, in vogue in the last score of years of the
seventeenth century, remained a feature of court dress,
and in a certain degree became once more part of ordinary
fashionable attire with the introduction of the bustle modes
alluded to (Plates LIX., LXI.). The petticoat, worn over
the hoop, had, like the skirt, pocket-holes concealed in the

side-gathers, and from about the middle of the century was frequently quilted (Plate LIV. B).[1]

GOWNS.—With the temporary suppression of the bustle (before 1720) the loose-bodied *sack* (Plate XLVIII. ; Plate L. ; Plate LI. D, E, H ; Fig. 94, A ; Fig. 118, B) became the characteristic fashionable gown until the 'forties. It was worn either open or closed in front, and might be sleeveless (as in Plate XLVIII. and—almost certainly—

FIG. 105.—French. *c.* 1735.

Fig. 118). At first hanging loose behind, the sack in the 'thirties merges into the *robe à la française*, the gown with the misnamed " Watteau pleats " (which, in their fully developed form, are never found in Watteau's pictures). In this the fullness behind is formally stitched at the top into regular box-pleats, which die away into the ample skirt of the gown (see, in particular, Plate L. E, and Fig. 115, C, D). The body may either fit loosely or mould the waist (being then made with a stiff foundation back and front, and sometimes laced under the back-pleats—see PATTERNS). In front it may be open the whole way down, or to the middle only (Plate LII. C ; Plate LIII. C ; Fig. 104), and may be laced, clasped, or otherwise fastened. A broad pleat sometimes edges the fronts. There is a tendency from about 1770 to sew the box-pleats flat to the back ; but for court functions at least the *robe à la française*, with its full pleats, persists until the Revolution.

Throughout the period we meet with a variety of gowns

[1] The petticoat worn under the hoop is referred to under LINEN : the pockets. under HOOPS, etc.

without the back-pleats (Fig. 106, D). Very fashionable from the 'seventies, though less ceremonious than the *robe à la française,* is the *polonaise,* with its rounded open fronts curving away to the back. It has a close-fitting body, and full skirts looped up by vertical running strings behind the hips into three overlapping festoons (Figs. 110, 111). There are also " made-up " *polonaises,* actually *cut* into festoons, the cords or ribbons being mere ornament.

From about 1750 full skirts, whether belonging to the

A.- B.

C. -D.

c. 1730.

1749.

FIG. 106.—A and B, French ; C and D, English.

gown or not, are often tucked under and drawn out through the pocket-holes, producing, of themselves, much of the projection of paniers (Fig. 115, A, B). Paniers may, of course, be worn in addition.[1]

HOOPS, BUSTLES, ETC.—After nearly a century's oblivion [2] the hooped petticoat reappears about 1710–15. At first

---

[1] Between 1710–60 a certain severity, or at least restraint, is evident in the matter of trimmings, but later fashions, particularly for full dress, are frequently overladen with tasteless ornament. During the 'eighties, in England especially, a reaction is visible in the simple muslin dresses—plain or striped, full in the skirts, with natural waists sashed with long broad ribbons—which grew in favour for every-day wear.

[2] Except for the seventeenth-century *guardinfanta* fashion in Spain and its dependencies.

funnel-shaped, it assumes in the 'twenties a broad cupola-form (Fig. 106, A), which is increasingly flattened at front and back till, from about the 'forties, its spread is almost entirely lateral (Plates L., LII., LIII., LIV., LV., LVII.; Figs. 104, 105, 107, B, D; 108 B, C, etc.). To pass through narrow openings a lady had to double her hoop together in front (Fig. 108, A) or move sideways. Hence about 1750 —or earlier—it is divided into two frames (*side-hoops*), like

FIG. 107.—English.

fire-guards tied about the waist (Fig. 109, A), with pocket-holes on the hips (Fig. 109, D), and bag-like pockets inside. A trifle later appears a hinged frame of metal, whereby the hoop could be lifted under the arms (Fig. 109, B, C). Connecting tapes held the metal arches at the required angle. In the 'seventies and 'eighties the hoops, except for court dress, tend to be supplanted once more by the bustle (*tournure*— Figs. 113, D; 116). Both vanished during the Revolution.

COATS, JACKETS, ETC.—Coats and waistcoats adapted from masculine patterns were no novelty (see Chapter V.): they continued in use for riding and hunting (Fig. 105).

Towards 1780 a wave of *anglomanie* brought into France
the English fashion of riding-coats with collars, lapels and

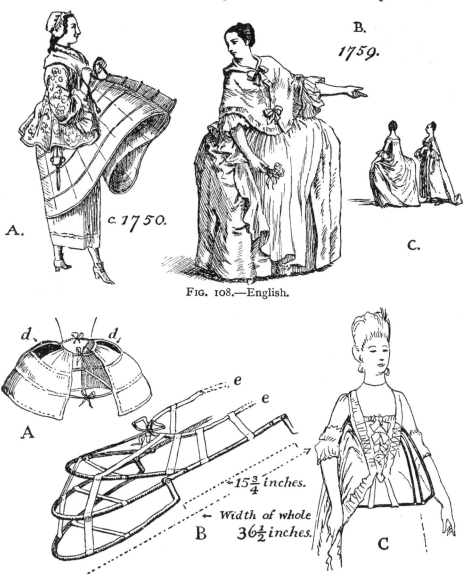

FIG. 108.—English.

FIG. 109.—Side-hoops, after Leloir.

capes, the skirts long or short, full or cut away (Fig. 117,
A, B, C), and the back-pleats, with their accompaniment

FIG. 110.—*Polonaises.* French.

FIG. 111.—*Polonaises.* A and B (*c.* 1778), French; C, English

of buttons and pocket-flaps, also borrowed from the masculine coat. Loose undress jackets with short sleeves (Fig. 108, A) occur throughout the greater part of the period; and abridgments of the gown and *polonaise* (*caraco à la française—caraco à la polonaise*—Fig. 113) were fashionable in the 'seventies and 'eighties.

CLOAKS, PELISSES, ETC.—Various forms of loose cloaklike wraps with arm-holes are found throughout for outdoor wear. Latterly the furred *pelisse*, with a broad collar or hanging hood (Fig. 114; Fig. 122, B) is the fashionable type. Scarves (Plate LI. I; Fig. 106, B) and hooded capes (Fig. 106, C; Fig. 107, B, C, E; Fig. 108, B; Fig. 112; Fig. 125, A) constantly appear in contemporary illustrations.

HEAD-GEAR.—The *fontange* was obsolete, surviving only in certain backwaters, and no caps or other headcoverings were worn for state occasions except by widows and elderly dames. For everyday wear caps of lace or fine linen were very fashionable till about the 'fifties: small at first, and arranged so as to expose the back of the head (Plate XLVIII. B; Fig. 118); sometimes with lappets at side or back, which might be pinned up to the crown (Plate L. C, D; Plate LII. B, etc.); sometimes, especially in the 'forties, with a little dip over the brow, reminiscent of the " Mary Queen of Scots " head-dress (Plate LIII. B). Elderly ladies and the *bourgeoisie* generally wore them larger; and about 1760 all caps began to grow in height or width, or both. Thenceforward till the end of the period they followed the growth of the coiffure (Figs. III, B; 112, B; 114; 115, A). Drooping frilled edges increased in favour. The *dormeuse*, characteristic of the 'seventies, framed the face closely between curving ruched borders (Fig. 124).

An affectation of rusticity—fashionable in England from the 'thirties, in France under Marie Antoinette—introduced broad straw hats of " milkmaid " type. In the first half of the period they were often worn over the small caps, and could be tied under the chin (Fig. 106, C, D; Fig. 107, A, B, C, E; Fig. 123). From the 'seventies there is

FIG. 112.—A, English; B, C and D, French.

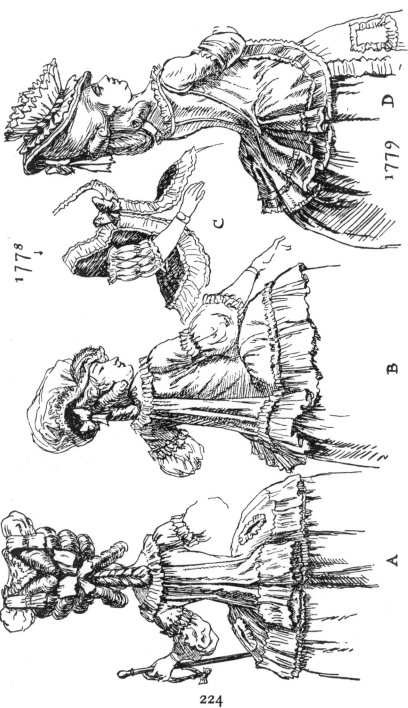

FIG. 113 —A and B, *Caracos à la française*; C and D, *Caracos à la polonaise.*

FIG. 114.—*Pelisses*. French. *c.* 1778.

no limit to the varieties of hats. They were tilted and cocked at every imaginable angle, and became much more ornate, with plumes, flowers, ribbons, fruit, and more ridiculous additions ; resembling modern millinery in their wide choice of material (Plate LIX. B, C ; Figs. 110, B ; 112, A ; 113, D ; 121, B). The student of their multiplicity of detail must perforce refer to the innumerable contemporary fashion-plates and satirical prints.

The masculine *tricorne* was occasionally used for riding

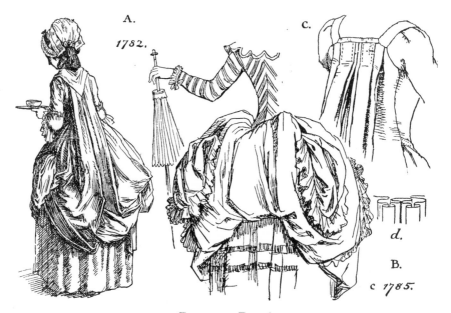

FIG. 115.—French.

and hunting (Fig. 105), and towards 1790 the broad wide-awake shape, of felt or beaver, with tall crown decorated with buckles and bows of ribbon, was adopted by sporting ladies (Fig. 117).

The small hood of the preceding period was retained with little modification (Fig. 106, A) as long as the hair was dressed closely, but the coiffures of the 'seventies and 'eighties called forth proportionate coverings such as the *calash*—a vast hood on hinged hoops, which could be raised and lowered like the hood of a gig (Fig. 125, B, C) ; or the lighter *thérèse*, made of gauze or other thin stuff over wires or whalebone (Fig. 125, A).

HAIR.—Till about 1760 the hair is kept close to the head and dressed off the face in front. A few informal curls are worn at the side, and the rest forms a small "bun" at the back (Plate XLVIII. B ; Plates L.–LIII., etc. ;

1788.

FIG. 116.—*Robe à l'anglaise.* French.

Fig. 94, A ; Fig. 106, B ; Fig. 118, etc.). Powder is always worn for full dress and usually on other occasions. Sometimes a few locks are allowed to hang at the nape (Fig. 104 ; Fig. 106, C, D ; Fig. 118, A) and—particularly for court wear—one or two of these may be brought forward over the shoulder,[1] a fashion of constant occurrence later on (Fig.

[1] Cf. Nattier's " Mme. Henriette " (with bass-viol) and " Marie Joseph de Saxe " at Versailles.

120). Towards 1760 the hair is dressed higher, and in the 'sixties becomes a tall egg-shaped structure with formal arrangements of curls (Plate LVII.). The pads used in these coiffures are supplemented in the 'seventies by cotton-wool foundations and masses of false hair until the size of the erection approaches the incredible. After 1775, a crazy elaboration is the key-note (see the later illustrations

FIG. 117.—A, B and C, English; D, French.

generally): the head is cumbered with stiff roll-curls, ribbons, feathers, flounces, bands, scarves, and, to crown all, with models of ships, coaches, windmills, and the like in blown glass, straw, etc. About 1780 the apex grows square and broad, and there is a general effort after width rather than height. Meanwhile the back hair usually hangs in a great chignon or in a catogan ; or again in long flowing curls. For undress in the 'eighties a full curly crop over the crown and very long hair behind were fashionable (Plate

FIG. 118.—French.

FIG. 119.—French.

LXII. A; Fig. 116; Fig. 122, B), and for informal occasions powder was more often discarded or sparingly employed.

A   B

c. 1785.   *c. 1775.*

FIG. 120.—A, English; B, French.

LINEN, ETC.—The chemise up to 1760–70 seldom shows more than a tiny frill above the *corsage*. Deep lace ruffles,

—1779—   *1776—*

a.   *b.*   *c.*

FIG. 121.—French.

often double or treble, hang from under the short sleeves. As already remarked, the *décolletage* is as often as not

FIG. 122.—English.

FIG. 123.—English.

partially or wholly masked by scarves or kerchiefs, whose ends are for the most part tucked into the bosom. Towards 1790 the *bouffant*—a curious full fichu covering the neck and bulging in pouter-pigeon style from the breast of the bodice —is fashionable (Plate LXII. A; Fig. 116); and about the same time broad-frilled collars are sometimes set about the shoulders. Tiny ruffs (Plate LVII.; Fig. 107, D) sometimes take the place of the close bands of ribbon at the throat,

FIG. 124.—A, English; B, German.

which are usual from about 1730 onwards (Figs. 104; 112, A, B; 121, B; 122, A). When masculine modes are worn, the appropriate neck-wear—stock, *jabot*, or cravat—is adopted with them (Fig. 105; Fig. 117, B, C).

The narrow under-petticoat worn with the great hoop is seen in Plate LII. B; Fig. 107, D; and Fig. 108, A.

SHOES.—Very tall " Louis " heels continue to be worn until the Revolution, but from about 1760 one notes a tendency towards lower heels for undress. After that date the high fronts and side latchets are seldom seen.

Buckles are ornate ; not infrequently they are replaced by ribbon-ties or rosettes (Figs. 107, D ; 112, A). In the second half of the century the toes are less acutely pointed. Satin, brocade and similar materials are used. *Mules* (Fig. 94, A) and riding-buskins (Fig. 117, D) still occur ; boots but rarely.

ACCESSORIES.—Long gloves of light-coloured silk or kid (Plate LIX. B ; Fig. 110, B ; Fig. 111, B ; Fig. 125, B) and silk or lace mittens (Fig. 107, B ; Fig. 112, B) are worn throughout the century. Short driving-gloves follow the

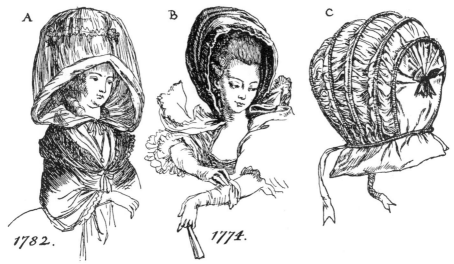

A

B

C

1782.

1774.

FIG. 125.—French.

masculine fashion (Fig. 117, A, B). From the 'seventies tall canes and parasols are often carried (Fig. 110, A ; Fig. 113, A ; Fig. 115, B ; Fig. 117, B). Laced and fringed aprons (Plate LV. ; Fig. 107, A, B) are of less frequent occurrence after the 'fifties. Flowers, real or artificial, are worn in the hair and at the bosom : no novel fashion, but encouraged by the eighteenth century patronage of " nature." Muffs (Fig. 106, B) outlive the century. Powder and paint are almost *de rigueur* at court, the powdered coiffure being held to kill the most florid complexion ; and with them the patch survives till the Revolution.

EUROPEAN COSTUME AND FASHION

NOTES ON THE ILLUSTRATIONS

PLATE XLVIII.—Contrast the relatively " modern " appearance of the yokel, A, with C, the man of fashion. The central figure shows the cut of the shirt.

PLATE XLIX.—Almost photographic in precision of detail. Observe the waistcoat sleeve of D ; and how the open fronts of the coat (A) and waistcoat (C) sag over the buttons—a characteristic feature of the 'twenties.

PLATE L.—This and the following plate are perfect illustrations of ultra-fashionable society in 1731.

PLATE LI.—Note the buttoned pleats of the coat-skirts in A. The same feature is observable in Plate L. B ; and Figs. 93 and 97. The men wear swords.

PLATE LII.—Note in B one way of manipulating the hoop; in C the upward curve of the hoop at the sides (cf. Figs. 104, 107, D), which is not characteristic of the second half of the century. The pictures in the background are full of suggestive detail (*e.g.* the crushed-up hoop of the lady in the sedan) and will repay closer study in the original print.

PLATES LIII.–LIV. show transitions in style. The split and buttoned sleeve of LIII. E has been noticed in the text of Chapter V.

PLATE LVII.—Note the angularity of the side-hoops or paniers.

PLATE LVIII.—An example of full *toilette d'apparat*, marked by a superfluity of trimmings and by exaggerated width in the paniers. The mantle with *fleurs-de-lis* is, of course, peculiar to royalty.

PLATE LIX.—Ordinary court dress. Note the *coiffure* and the profusion of jewellery.

PLATE LXI.—The *sans-gêne* of the gentlemen's costume is accounted for by their character as patrons of the notorious Madame Cornelys' assembly-rooms.

PLATE LXII.—There is a note of simplicity in this fashionable undress. The lady's *corsage* is laced across, and there is already a hint of the high " Empire " waist. In B observe the set of the coat collar, and the shoe-strings in place of buckles.

PLATE LXIII.—A fine, comprehensive view of the walking-dress of the better classes.

FIG. 88.—This (in C) and Fig. 90, A, show the strap and buckle at the nape for adjusting the fit of the wig. In D and E it will be seen that the bows on the bag are merely ornamental. D shows the *solitaire* ribbon.

234

PLATE XLVIII.

FRENCH. 1721.

A   B   C

"GERSAINT'S SIGNBOARD"—(LEFT HALF).   *Watteau.*

COLLEGIUM MEDICUM.

A   B   C   D   E

C. Troost.

A   B   C   D   E   F   G

DÉCLARATION D'AMOUR.   *J. F. de Troy.*

PLATE LI.

FRENCH. 1731.

F

A B C D E G H I J

MME. MERCIER AND FAMILY.   *J. Dumont.*

TASTE IN HIGH LIFE. S. *Phillips* (*after Hogarth*).

PLATE LIII.

ENGLISH. 1749.

A   B   C   D   E

FAMILY GROUP.   J. Wills.

245

Fig. 89.—Compare the arrangement of hanging locks at the back of A and B (*perruque à nœuds*) with Fig. 93.

Fig. 92.—D wears a wig which distinguishes him as a member of a learned profession. Contrast its comparative severity with B and C.

Fig. 93.—The hip-buttons are far apart : contrast with the later examples, 96, C, D. See also note, Fig. 89.

Fig. 94.—C is a constructional sketch of the split turn-back cuff. The lady apparently wears a diminutive cap : her sack is buttoned from breast to feet (cf. Fig. 118, B).

Fig. 96.—Maccaroni modes : cf. Fig. 100, B, C, E, F, G. The *jabot* is shown with greater clearness in *a* than in the complete figure A.

Fig. 97.—A French adaptation of English fashion. The hat is called a *bavaroise* : the coat, *redingote anglaise*.

Fig. 98.—Though a little beyond our period, this figure serves as well for 1790.

Fig. 99.—A shows an actual coat and hat in the collection of M. Maurice Leloir. C is a back view of a hat similar to A, B.

Fig. 102 may represent either boots or spatterdashes (see Chapter V., text).

Fig. 103.—Specimens of top-boots, showing the bracing straps. D is a post-boy's boot. Observe the characteristic hat-trimming of bows and buckled ribbons. The fashion of fastening back the coat skirts for riding (B) is chiefly military. E is an early double-breasted waistcoat.

Fig. 106.—In B the scarf is crossed in front and the ends knotted behind as in Plate LI. 1.

Fig. 108.—B and C show the difference between the narrow side view of the hoop and the width as seen from front or back.

Fig. 115.—C and *d* are constructional drawings of the box-pleats of the *robe à la française*, from an actual specimen in the Victoria and Albert Museum.

Fig. 116.—Distinctive dress for little boys comes in about this date. The type illustrated is modelled on sailors' costume.

Fig. 124.—In A, the lappets are tied under the chin : in B, pinned up. B is of a more *bourgeois* character in general. Cf. modifications of *dormeuse*, Figs. 114, 115, A.

Fig. 125.—C is from a specimen in the Victoria and Albert Museum.

PLATE LIV.

ENGLISH. 1729.

ENGLISH. c. 1750.

ENGLISH. c. 1750.

A

SIR THOS. PENN.

Ph. van Dyck.

B

LADY PENN.

Ph. van Dyck.

C

EARL OF SALISBURY.

Highmore.

249

INFANTA MARIE ISABELLE. *Nattier.*

MME. DE POMPADOUR.   *Q. la Tour.*

ARCHDUCHESS MARIA JOSEPHA.   *R. Mengs.*

255

MARIE ANTOINETTE. *Callet.*

ARCHDUCHESS MARIA CHRISTINA. *J. Zoffany.*

A   B   C   *Gainsborough.*

DUKE AND DUCHESS OF CUMBERLAND AND LADY ELIZABETH LUTTERELL (DETAIL).

PLATE LXI.

ENGLISH. 1781.

A   B   C   D

PROMENADE AT CARLISLE HOUSE.   *J. R. Smith.*

A B

SIR WM. AND LADY TWYSDEN. *J. Downman.*

PLATE LXIII

ENGLISH. 1790.

VIEW OF BUCKINGHAM HOUSE (DETAIL).

E. Dayes

PATTERNS

PLATES LXIV. TO LXIX.

LIST OF PATTERNS

PAGE

PLATE LXIV. FIG. 1—CLOAK WITH HANGING SLEEVES, c. 1560; FIG. 2—
SPANISH CAPE, c. 1570; FIG. 3—SHOULDER-PUFFS OF LADY'S
GOWN, c. 1560 271

PLATE LXV. FIG. 1—PEASECOD DOUBLET AND TRUNK-HOSE, c. 1580;
FIG. 2—VENETIANS, c. 1585 273

PLATE LXVI. FIG. 1—BODICE AND STOMACHER, WITH (FIG. 2) BODY OF
OVER-DRESS, c. 1625–30 274

PLATE LXVII. FIG. 1—DOUBLET AND BREECHES, c. 1640; FIG. 2—
DOUBLET, c. 1620 275

PLATE LXVIII. FIGS. 1 AND 2—COAT, WAISTCOAT AND BREECHES OF
c. 1730 277

PLATE LXIX. FIG. 1—ROBE À LA FRANÇAISE, c. 1770; FIGS. 2 AND 3—
DETAILS OF ITS CONSTRUCTION 278

N.B.—The scale of measurement is given wherever known.

Plate LXIV.

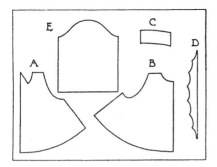

FIG. 1.—Pattern of cloak with
hanging sleeves, *c.* 1560.

A—front; B—back; C—half
of upright collar; D—shoulder-
wing; E—hanging sleeve.

(After KOEHLER.)

Broad lapels cut with a "step"; the
hanging cowl at back is the characteristic
feature of the *capa castellana* (Spanish cape).

(After KOEHLER.)

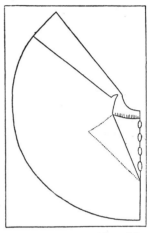

FIG. 2.—Half of "Spanish
cape" with hood, *c.* 1570.

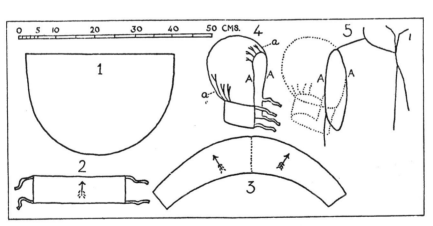

FIG. 3.—Shoulder-puff and standing collar of lady's loose gown, *c.* 1560.

1—Pattern of shoulder; 2—ditto of armband, tied with strings;
3—standing collar (the arrows indicate the direction of the "grain");
4—the completed shoulder-puff (*aa* = gathers: AA = limits of shoulder-
seam); 5—ditto in position. (After LELOIR.)

PLATE LXV. FIG. 1 (*opposite*)—

A—Front of slashed and puffed *peasecod* doublet.
B—Back of ditto.
C—Half of collar of ditto (**C'** shows whole collar wired to shape).
D—Half of skirt.
E—Sleeve (outer half).
F—Ditto (inner half).
G—Short trunks. The dotted line *aa* shows the overlap of the doublet skirt, the radiating lines indicate the slashing or *paning*. The dotted double cross-lines on the doublet indicate where the fullness is caught down between the puffs.

(After LELOIR.)

PLATE LXV. FIG. 2 (*opposite*)—

A—Front; **B**—back; **C**—half of waistband. *aa* indicate the gathers whereby the legs are fulled on to the waistband. The curious " bandy-legged " cut and the shape at the knee are important. It is this curve that gives the peculiar creases so characteristic of certain sixteenth-century figures by Goltzius and others.

(After LELOIR.)

Plate LXV.

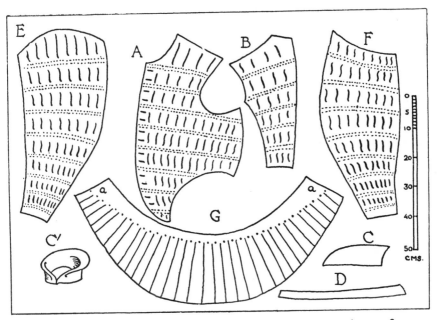

FIG. 1.—Puffed and slashed doublet and short trunks, French, *c.* 1580.

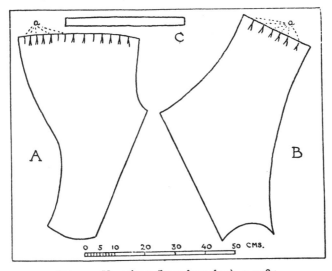

FIG. 2.—Venetians (knee-breeches), *c.* 1585.

273

Plate LXVI.

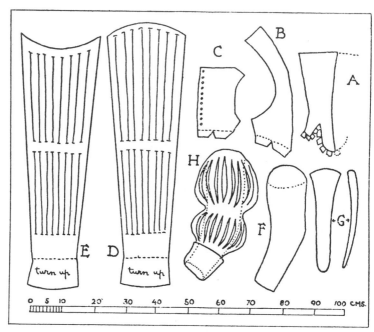

FIG. 1.—Lady's bodice and stomacher, *c.* 1625–30.

A—Half stomacher with border of looped tabs (pickadils) at base ; B—front of bodice ; C—back with eyelets for lacing ; D—outer half of slashed sleeve ; E—inner ditto ; F—foundation of sleeve ; G—front and profile views of wooden busk, lining the stomacher ; H—shows appearance of sleeve when padded and mounted on F. Note the turn-up cuff.

(After LELOIR.)

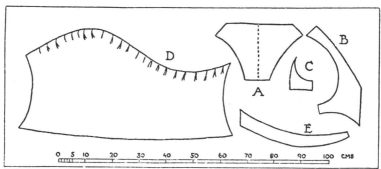

FIG. 2.—Body of lady's gown worn over the bodice preceding.

A—Back ; B—front ; C—side ; D—full elbow-sleeve, gathered along top edge and open down front ; E—wing.

(After LELOIR.)

Plate LXVII.

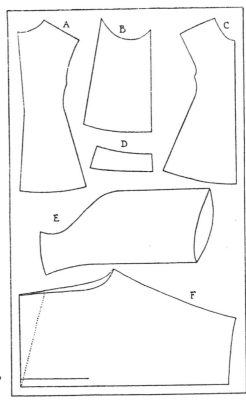

FIG. I.—

    A — back ;   **B** — side ;
C—front ; **D**—half collar ;
E—sleeve ; **F**—breeches.

        (After MASSNER.)

FIG. I.—Doublet and breeches,
c. 1640.

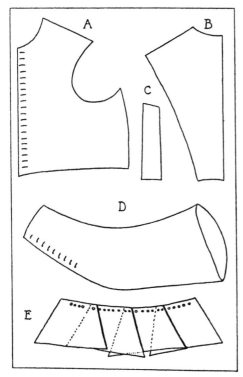

FIG 2.—

    A — front ;   **B** — back ;
C—half collar ; **D**—sleeve ;
E—skirt of overlapping tabs.
In this instance the usual
" wings " are missing.

        (After MASSNER.)

FIG. 2.—Late Jacobean (early
Louis XIII.) doublet.

PLATE LXVIII. FIG. I (*opposite*)—

A—Front; B—back; C—sleeve, outer half; D—ditto, inner half , E—outer half of cuff; F—inner half of ditto; G—collar-strip; H—pocket flap (note in A the actual *triangular* opening of the pocket itself). *a* and *b* are gussets added to skirts of A and B respectively, as indicated in dotted lines. The radiating side-pleats of the skirts are indicated by dotted lines. In C and D the marks × × indicate the starting-point of the split cuff.

N.B.—The *front* skirts are interlined with buckram or parchment to make them "flare." Note the arrow-heads indicating the direction of the "grain." The fit of the coat is loose in front, but *skin-tight* behind from nape to waist.

(After LELOIR.)

PLATE LXVIII. FIG. 2 (*opposite*)—

Waistcoat: A—front (the skirts are buckramed); B—back, with eyelet-holes to lace up centre; C—sleeve, outer half; D—ditto, inner half; E—pocket-flap; F—collar strip (it should be noted that, despite this added strip, both coats and collars at this date are cut rather *décolleté* or wide-necked in front: *i.e.* if buttoned at top they would by no means reach the throat). In B, C and D the parts of both sleeve and back below the dotted line match the front of the waistcoat. The button-holes are rarely more numerous than this, and that at the top is rarely used for fear of crushing the *jabot*, although *dummy* buttonholes and buttons run from neck to waist.

Breeches: A—front; B—back; C—waistband; D, E, F—gussets and flaps; G—garter. These breeches are made very full on seat and gathered behind into waistband. The legs fit closely and button with six buttons above the garter or knee-strap. *a* shows their general appearance when made up.

Plate LXVIII.

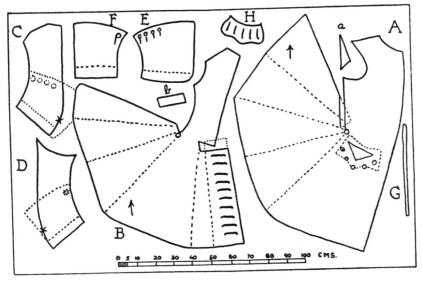

FIG. I.—A coat of *c.* 1730.

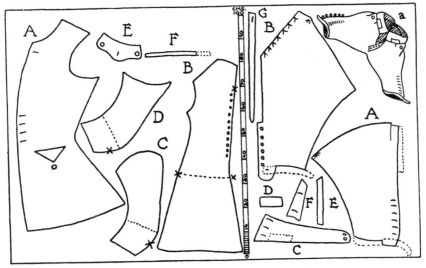

FIG. 2.—Waistcoat and breeches to accompany the preceding.

277

Plate LXIX.

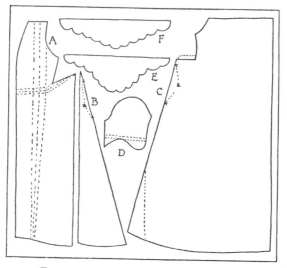

FIG. 1.—A *robe à la française, c.* 1770.

A — front ; the vertical dotted lines indicate gathers, those running across waist tucks, to allow the skirt to flare over the hoop. Well marked above the waist, the gathers fade to nothing below. B—side ; C—back, note extent of pocket-hole (*a*) indicated by curved dotted line ; D—elbow-sleeve, to which are sewn flounces E and F, the latter uppermost.

A — front ; B — back ; C—gathers at hips ; D—fullness on hips relaxed.

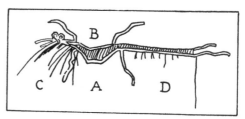

FIG. 2 —Skirt of *robe à la française*, showing arrangement at hips.

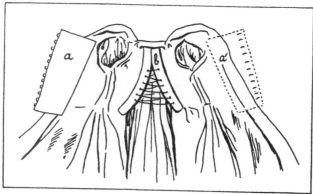

FIG. 3.—Construction of body of *robe à la française*.

Inside view showing the false fronts or *compères* (*a* and *a'*) and the stiffening and lacing at the back under the so-called "Watteau pleat." Cf. fig. 115.

COSTUMES

PLATES LXX. TO LXXVI.

COSTUMES OF DIVERSE PERIODS : either original, partly restored, or accurately reconstructed by experts from contemporary patterns and data. COIFFURES, BODY-LINEN, STOCKINGS, ETC., mostly copied from old models, and in old materials.

COSTUMES

PAGE

PLATE LXX. A.—A doublet (c. 1575) and paned trunks (1610) in the Metropolitan Museum, New York, by courtesy of late Dr. Bashford Dean; the latter from a castle in the Carpathians, and depicted (B) in a portrait of 1610 *ibidem* . . . 281

PLATE LXXI. A.—Two doublets (English) of c. 1620–30 of the same type as Plates XXXI. A and B, XXXII., and Fig. 59. Victoria and Albert Museum 282

PLATE LXXI. B.—Doeskin " arming doublet," the shoulders and skirts quilted with gold thread for wear under armour; and iron skeleton lining for an ordinary hat. Italian (c. 1570). By courtesy of Cyril Andrade, Esq. 282

PLATE LXXII.—French lady (c. 1625–30) and gentleman (c. 1635), from the collections of the Société de l'Histoire du Costume, Paris 283

PLATE LXXIII. A.—Breeches of the Isham wedding suit (1681). English. See footnote, p. 161. Victoria and Albert Museum 284

PLATE LXXIII. B.—Doeskin coat (with silver " Persian " embroidery) and jack-boots (c. 1680). London Museum . . . 284

PLATE LXXIV.—French gentleman and little boy (c. 1730). The patterns of Plate LXVIII. are from A. B is dressed in Hungarian style, a common mode for French children, as our Victorians used sailor suits and Highland costume. Société de l'Histoire du Costume 285

PLATE LXXV. A.—Full-skirted coat (c. 1720) and waistcoat (c. 1700). English. Victoria and Albert Museum . . . 286

PLATE LXXV. B.—Sack or gown with so-called " Watteau back " (*robe à la française*) of c. 1735–40. English. Victoria and Albert Museum 286

PLATE LXXVI.—French lady and gentleman (c. 1765). Société de l'Histoire du Costume, Paris 287

B

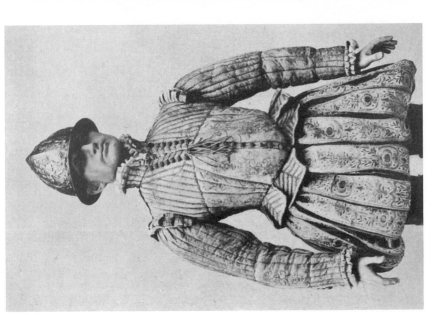

A

A. DOUBLET OF *c.* 1575 AND TRUNKHOSE OF 1610; the latter are the original of those shown in the portrait (B) of an Austrian noble.—*Metropolitan Museum, New York.*

PLATE LXXI

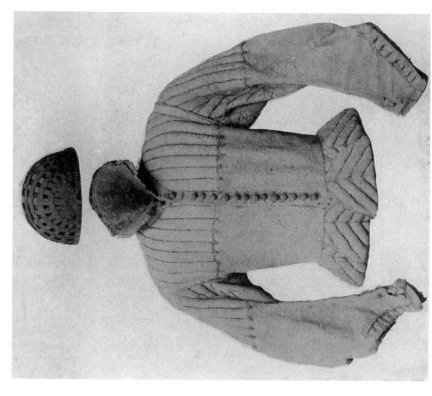

B. DOESKIN DOUBLET, the shoulders and skirts quilted for wear

A. TWO DOUBLETS (English)
of c. 1620–30, of same type as

282

PLATE LXXII.

LADY (*c.* 1625–30) AND GENTLEMAN (*c.* 1635). French.—*From collections of Société de l'Histoire du Costume, Paris.*

PLATE LXXIII.

DOESKIN COAT WITH SILVER "PERSIAN"
EMBROIDERY AND JACKBOOTS.
_____ _____ London Museum.

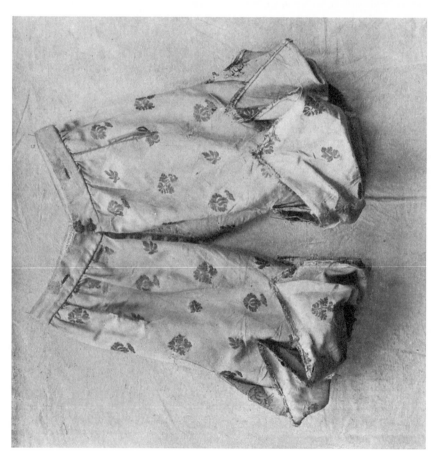

BREECHES OF THE ISHAM WEDDING SUIT, 1681 (English).
(*See foot-note, page* 161.)

Plate LXXIV.

French Gentleman and Little Boy.   c. 1730.
The patterns of Plate LXVIII. are from the former;
the child is in Hungarian dress, a common children's
fashion in France, like our Victorian sailor's suits and
Highland dresses.

Société de l'Histoire du Costume, Paris.

PLATE LXXV.

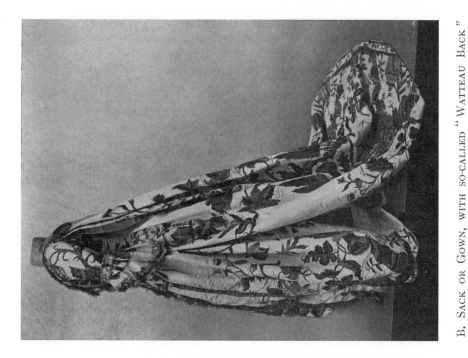

B. SACK OR GOWN, WITH SO-CALLED "WATTEAU BACK"

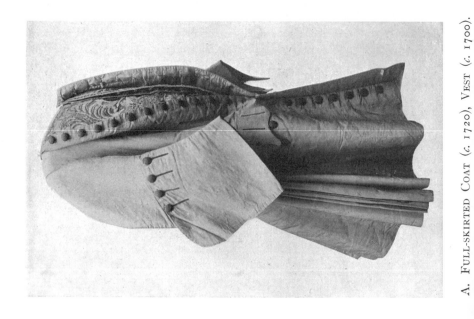

A. FULL-SKIRTED COAT (c. 1720), VEST (c. 1700).

Plate LXXVI.

French Lady and Gentleman (*c.* 1765).

Société de l'Histoire du Costume, Paris.

ADDENDA

Introduction, p. x.—*A propos* of conservatism in attire, note how elderly folk throughout tended to adhere to the fashions of their prime.

——, p. xi.—In examining old materials due allowance must of course be made for the fading of the dyes.

Chapter I., p. 8 (Slashes).—The soft underlying material is often " drawn out " in great puffs (*pullings out*) through the slashes.

Chapter II., p. 39.—The relative lengths of upper- and nether-stock vary greatly ; the upper-stock may merely cover the hips or reach below the knee. The term *breech* begins to be transferred to the upper part of the long hose. The codpiece is at its most obtrusive *c.* 1510–1575 (Plates IX. A, XIV. B ; Figs. 12, 32). Note that the old sewn or tailored nether-stocks are cut " on the cross " or bias-wise. Exaggerated codpieces are rare outside France, England, and the Netherlands.

——, p. 46.—The long ornamental fronts (or *chaffers*) of the gable-hood are turned up level with the ear-lobes from the 'twenties, and the ends folded over the crown (Plate VII. ; Figs. 19, 21). Except (till the late 'sixties) for old ladies, the gable grows unfashionable from *c.* 1540. It was always a strictly national mode ; the " rolls " vanished with it. Its place was taken by the type of French hood shown in portraits of Catherine Howard, who perhaps sponsored the new vogue.

Chapter III., p. 54 (Introductory).—In Italy, Venice in particular evolved a style largely her own, while in the Two Sicilies and the Milanese the gentry followed Spain. In Germany most of the great Catholic lords (notably the Hapsburgs) and their following were Spanish in habits and sympathies, in contrast to the Protestant princes.

——, p. 55 (Doublets).—The waist-line, independent of the peasecod fashion, gradually sinks from 1560–80 to an ever deeper point in front (Plate XVI. B). From the 'nineties comes in a skirt of spreading tabs overlapping backwards and drooping forward to a point.

——, p. 57 (Jerkin).—The jerkin sometimes has deep skirts almost covering the trunks ; from *c.* 1600 it is often of overlapping flaps. Where it has hanging sleeves, these are sometimes twisted together or tucked into the girdle behind. Sometimes the jerkin matches the breeches and contrasts with the doublet in pattern and material. The *chamarre* was a jerkin thickly criss-crossed with lace, braid, etc., which was sometimes mounted on coarse stuff and the ground then cut away, leaving an open design of strap-work. The panes of the trunk-hose might be similarly *chamarrés*.

Chapter III., p. 60 (Trunk-hose).—The type of trunks gradually widening to the base—ever a favourite in Spain—prevails after *c.* 1575.

——, p. 63 (Breeches).—Breeches and doublet were united by *points*. Where the fastening is visible, as happens up to *c.* 1560 and often after 1610, it takes the form of a row of bows along the waist-line. After *c.* 1630 the points become a mere ornament and the breeches are hooked to the doublet. By the 'forties the breeches are mostly supported by their peculiar fit, and this is the case till far into the eighteenth century, though the first braces (*gallowses*) appear towards 1700.

——, p. 64 (Headgear).—The *copotain* or sugar-loaf crowned hat (Plate XVI. B; Fig. 33 C) was a form much in favour with the French Catholics of the Guise faction. In general the courtly head-gear is adorned with ostrich-tips (Plates XIII., XIV. A, XVI. B; Figs. 39, 40, 41 A) often topped with heron's plumes (Figs. 40, 41 C).

——, p. 71 (Gowns).—Throughout this period various loose "one-piece" gowns are worn, especially by elderly ladies. A typical form fastens only at the throat, opening in a $\wedge$ down the front and hanging funnel-like from the great, puffed shoulders.

Chapter IV., p. 121 (General Note).—The French edict of 1633 restraining the gentry from using embroidery, lace, and expensive trimmings generally, found some slight response in England. It endured for a couple of years, but corresponds with the perfection of the "Vandyke" modes.

——, p. 125 (Breeches).—Note that trunk-hose, though retained for *full court-dress* (and by elderly men) up to *c.* 1620, were little used after *c.* 1600 by beaux for ordinary wear. "Old Mr. Grice" is noted in an obituary of 1640 as one "who wore trunk breeches," a very freak of obsoletism.

——, p. 130.—Note how in festal attire the lace band is commonly worn *over* the cloak (Plate XXXV.; Fig. 64 A).

Chapter V., p. 159 (*re* the vest "after the Persian mode").—Since this book first appeared, a contemporary sketch from the M.S. *Journal* of the Earl of Sandwich, Pepys's patron, purporting (for it hardly bears out the descriptions by Pepys or Rugge) to depict this fashion, has been published in John Drinkwater's *Mr. Charles, King of England* (see p. ix). Possibly, too, Hollar's satirical etching, commonly known as "King Charles's cranes," of 1666 may refer to it. Randle Holme (1688) says it was borrowed from the dress of the *Russian embassy*.

——, p. 160.—*Cheats* were waistcoats having only the fronts of fine material, richly trimmed.

——, p. 161.—Till the second quarter of the seventeenth century

ADDENDA

Spaniards had been identified with wide, bombasted trunks. From that time " Spanish " breeches denotes skin-tight knickers close buttoned (8 to 10 buttons) at the knee.

Chapter V., p. 165.—The three-cornered hat in this and the following period was mostly carried under the arm, not to disorder the curled and powdered wig.

——, *ibid.*—One form of *montero* is akin to the helmet of modern airmen and motor-cyclists.

——, p. 167.—" Made-up " cravats were common as early as 1672.

——, p. 176.—A fully developed *fontange* figures as early as 1685 in M. Burghers' print of the old Ashmolean Museum.

——, p. 185.—In the *taure* or " bull-head " (*c.* 1674) the front hair was brought down on the brow in a close-curled mop.

Chapter VI., p. 199.—The *brigadier* wig (Fig. 89 C, D.), ending in two corkscrew curls at the nape, was often confused with the *major*, which by rights had but one such tail.

——, p. 203.—The spreading, stiffened-out coat-skirts dropped quite out of vogue after 1760. Till then coats had a rather *décolleté* cut.

——, p. 204.—For *gala* wear the coat-collar is often a single stand-up.

——, p. 207.—The waistcoats of *c.* 1715–1760 are tightened behind by strings or lacing. When the sleeved waistcoat is wholly of good material it may be worn indoors without the coat as a *négligé*.

——, p. 212 (Solitaire).—The *solitaire* might be independent of the wig-tie.

——, p. 216 (Gowns).—The *robe à l'anglaise* has a tight-fitted corset-bodice, and a full skirt (Fig. 116), like what used to be called a " princess robe."

BIBLIOGRAPHY

IN conjunction with the present work we would especially commend to
the reader :

FAIRHOLT, F. W. : *Costume in England.* (Dillon's edition of 1896.)
  (By far the best English handbook, and invaluable for its
  store of contemporary quotations.)
PARIS—SOCIÉTÉ DE L'HISTOIRE DU COSTUME :
  Bulletin. (2 vols.)
  Costumes et Uniformes.
    Periodical publications. Articles, fully illustrated, dealing
    fully with subject of Costume. Photographs and
    Patterns of actual Specimens.

DRESDEN—VEREIN FÜR HISTORISCHE . . . KOSTÜMKUNDE.
  (Similar in character to preceding.)

Admirable and copious illustrations from contemporary Art are
collected in :

HIRTH, GEORG : *Les Grands Illustrateurs.* (6 vols.)
Anon., Munich : *Historisch interessante Bildnisse und Trachten.*
DIEDRICHS : *Deutsches Leben der Vergangenheit.* (2 vols.)
BOEHN, MAX VON : *Die Mode . . . im XVI. Jahrhundert.*
  ,,   ,,   ,,   *XVII.*   ,,
  ,,   ,,   ,,   *XVIII.*   ,,
DIMIER, LOUIS : *Histoire de la peinture de portrait en France au
  XVIᵉ siècle.* 2 vols.
    (Contains an admirable selection of works of the " Clouet "
    school.)
MOREAU-NÉLATON : *Les Clouet et leurs emules.* 3 vols.
    (No less rich in illustrative matter.)
ROY, HIPPOLYTE : *La vie, la mode et le costume au XVIIᵉ siècle :
  époque Louis XIII.*
MASNER, KARL : *Kostümaustellung*; devoted to photographs (with
  patterns) of actual costumes.
SCHÉFER, GASTON : *Documents pour servir à l'histoire du costume,*
  etc.

293

BIBLIOGRAPHY

Galerie des modes. (Reprint.)
(The last two illustrate fashions of the second half of XVIIIth century.)
See also in *Magazine of Art,* Vols. XI. and XII., "Studies in English Costume," by Richard Heath. (Patterns, etc.)

The most important *general* treatises on Costume are :

ENGLISH

STRUTT, JOSEPH : *Dress and Habits,* etc.
(*The* pioneer treatise.)
PLANCHE, J. R. : *British Costume.*
  „   *Cyclopædia of Costume.*
(A standard work.)
CALTHROP, D. C. : *English Costume.*
(Lucid and to the point.)

FRENCH

JACQUEMIN, R. : *Iconographie du Costume.* (Plates only.)
LECHEVALLIER-CHEVIGNARD : *Costumes des XVIe, XVIIe, et XVIII siècles.* *
PITON, C. : *Costume civil en France.* *
QUICHERAT, J. : *Costume en France.*
(The standard French text-book.)
RACINET, A. : *Le Costume en France.* (Vols. IV. and V.)
(Most ambitious and comprehensive in scope and style, but of very unequal value.)
For the Middle Ages one cannot omit VIOLLET-LE-DUC'S works, C. ENLART'S *Manuel d'archéologie française—III. Le Costume ;* nor, for classified texts on the various headings, VICTOR GAY'S *Glossaire.*

GERMAN

FALKE, J. VON : *Kostümgeschichte der Kulturvölker.* * †
HEFNER-ALTENECK, J. VON : *Trachten.* *
HEYDEN, A. VON : *Blätter für Kostumkunde.*
(Fair, but scrappy.)
  „   „   *Tracht der Kulturvölker.*
HOTTENROTH, F. VON : *Handbuch der deutschen Tracht.* * †
(Very thorough, but really concentrates on Germany.)
  „   „   *Tracht,* etc.
(Most comprehensive, but not quite reliable.)
MÜNCHNER BILDERBOGEN. Zur Geschichte des Kostüms. (Plates only.)

* Illustrations good.   † Useful text.

294

BIBLIOGRAPHY

KÖHLER, KARL : *Trachten der Völker in Bild und Schnitt.** † ‡
KRETSCHMER, A., and ROHRBACH, K. : *Trachten der Völker.*
MÜTZEL, HANS : *Vom Lendenschurz zur Modentracht.** †
QUINCKE, W. : *Handbuch der Kostümkunde.*
 (A most handy pocket compendium and ideal manual for
     the tyro.)
ROSENBERG, C. A. : *Geschichte des Kostüms.*
SICHART, EMMA VON : *Praktische Kostümkunde.*
 (Adapted from Köhler's book, translated into English as
    A History of Costume, by A. K. Dallas.)
WEISS, HERMANN : *Kostümkunde.** †
 (Typically German in its thoroughness, but contains some
 ludicrous howlers, *e.g.* in rendering Old French texts.)

Periodicals such as the *Burlington Magazine, The Connoisseur,* and
in fact all publications dealing with Ancient Art and Antiquities generally,
should be glanced through wherever met for possible material. The
innumerable illustrated monographs, *catalogues raisonnés,* etc., so plenti-
ful nowadays, will yield endless stores of first-class information. Thus, to
take one instance, Mr. Collins Baker's *Lely and the Stuart Portrait-Painters*
is, within its limits, invaluable, and any amount of material offers in the
annual volumes of the Walpole Society. Illustrated catalogues of public
and private collections and of sales should not be overlooked.

It should be superfluous to refer the reader to the numerous works on
monumental effigies, brasses and the like, *e.g.* Stothard, Hollis, Prior and
Gardiner, Crossley, Boutell, Waller, Haines and a host of others to be found
in any good bibliography. For the XVth century, France and (conse-
quently) England, were so much indebted to the Low Countries for much
of their art and civilisation, that the splendid school that gathered round
the Dukes of Burgundy affords a mine of information. Before venturing
upon Chapter I., we would therefore advise the beginner to look up the
section " Lancaster and York " in Fairholt's work, and for its better
illustration such a work as Fierens-Gevaert's *Les Primitifs Flamands,*
with special reference to the works of the Van Eycks, Petrus Cristus,
Rogier van der Weyden, Thierry Bouts, Hugo van der Goes and Memlinc.
The miniatures of XVth century MSS. are also invaluable. The four
centuries preceding the period of this book will be found very fully
treated in Mr. Herbert Norris's *Costume and Fashion,* vol. ii.

N.B.—All works above enumerated, and many more, will be found at
the British Museum or Victoria and Albert Museum National Art Library.
Actual albums of contemporary costumes date from the second half of
the XVIth century, *e.g.* : Bertelli, Weigel, Boissard, de Bruyn, Vecellio,§

---

* Illustrations good.   † Useful text.   ‡ Dress patterns.
 § Vecellio's is the first containing descriptive notices (Lacombe's French trans-
lations of these in Didot's edition of 1859–63 are inadequate), and, with Boissard and
Bruyn, the most reliable.

BIBLIOGRAPHY

Franco, etc. Braun & Hogenberg's topographical work, *Civitates orbis terrarum*, is another mine of information. Genuine *fashion-plates* appear from the XVIIth century with accompanying text. Tailors' pattern-books are found as early as the XVIth century, *e.g.* ALCEGA, *Geometria y traça*, Seville, 1588, which contains patterns and directions for cutting doublets, jerkins, cloaks, verdingales, etc., in abundance.

A remarkably full bibliography of costume, armour, and all related subjects is the catalogue of the famous costume-library of Franz, Baron von LIPPERHEIDE, now an annexe of the Kunstgewerbe Museum, Berlin. (Copy in the Victoria and Albert Museum, National Art Library.)

INDEX AND GLOSSARY

Reference to the page is made in ordinary Arabic numerals, to the inset line illustrations in italicised Arabic figures, and to plates in Roman numerals.

Items of such general character as boots, stockings, cloaks, hairdressing, etc., being duly discussed under their proper headings in the text, have been ignored here.

AGLET or AIGLET (Fr. *aiguillette*)—The metal tag of a POINT, xi, 8, 11, 13, 14, 17, 44, *8*, *14*, *19*, *24*, *32*, *33* E, *59*, *61*, *66* A, B, *66* B, VI., XXI., XXVII. A.

ANGLOMANIE—219.

APRON—185, XLV. B.

BAG-WIG—199, *88*, L. B., LII. D.

BALDRICK—131, 169, *59–61*, *71* B, *72*, *73*, *75*, XL.

BAND—Collar of linen or lace, generally = Falling-band, in opposition to RUFF (*q.v.*), 67, 78, 130, 167, *26* A, B, *38*, *40*, *61* C, *64*, *71* B, *73*, *74* B, XVIII., XXII., XXXII.–XXXV., XXXVII.–XL., XLIII.

BASES—Skirts of jerkin, sometimes independent, 6, 35, IV. B, V. B, X, XI. B, D.

BAVAROISE—*See* note on p. 247, and Fig. *97*.

BIBLIOGRAPHY—299.

BOMBAST—Padding or stuffing, especially cotton-wool or flocks, 54.

BOOT-HOSE—Thick over-stockings, mostly worn inside riding-boots and over the ordinary stockings; about 1640–60 sometimes with shoes, 64, 125, 162, *65–66*, *72*, *75*, XXXVII. B and D.

BREECHES—Originally in one with the stockings, or sewn to them; afterwards a separate garment, 64.

BRIGADIER WIG—*89* C, D., 297.

BUCKLES (on shoes)—166, 210, 223, *76*, *80*, XLV.–XLVI., XLIX., LIV., LX. A.

BUFF-COAT, BUFF-JERKIN—One of stout leather, especially ox hide, 124, *60*, XXXIV. A and E, XXXVII. B and F.

BUSKIN—166 (footnote).

BUSTLE—*See* CUL DE PARIS and TOURNURE, 174, 218, *113* D, *116*.

CALASH—226, *125* B and C.

CANIONS—Tubular extensions of the short, bombasted breeches to the knee or below, 63, *26* C, *28*, *33* A and D, *48* B, XVI., XVIII., XIX.

CANNONS—Frills, ruches, or similar gathered trimmings at the knees of the breeches; or the wide tops of long stockings drawn up over the breeches;

also PORT-CANNONS, 162, 186, *73*, XXXIX., XLIII. A.

CARACO—222, *113*.

CASSOCK—157, *72*.

CATOGAN or CLUB—200, *90* A, B, *100* B, C, *101* B, C.

CHAMARRE—295.

CHAPE—The ferrule or tip of a scabbard, the metal mouthpiece (and other mounts) being known as a LOCKET.

CHEATS—296.

CLOG or PATTEN, 130, *66* B, C.

COAT—158, 203, *71* C, *74–76*, *93–94*, *98*, *102*, XLII., XLIV.–XLVIII. C, XLIX.–LIV.

COCK—Manner of looping up the hat-brim, the origin of the three-cornered and modern "cocked" hats.

CODPIECE (Fr. *braguette*)—A feature of breeches down to *c.* 1580; page 11, 63 and illustrations *passim*.

COMMODE or FONTANGE—176, *83* A, *87*, XLV. B.

COPOTAIN HAT—296,

CRAVAT—167, 212, *72*, *74* A, *75*, *76*, *78*, *98*, *100* C, F, XL. B, XLII. A, XLIV.–XLVII., XLIX.

CRAVAT-STRING—Originally a ribbon for tying the cravat at the throat; later a mere garnish of ribbons, *74* A, *75*, *78* A, XL. B, XLII. A, XLV. A.

CROSS-GARTERS—64, *34*, *36*, XVI. A.

CUFF—Originally the turned-up wristband of the shirt; afterwards the turned-up end or facing of the sleeve, 68, 130, 159, 204, *74–76*, *79*, *93–95*, XXXIV. H, XXXVIII. C, XLII.–XLVII., XLIX., LIV.

CUL DE PARIS—Early form of BUSTLE; see TOURNURE, 174, 218, *113* D, *116*.

DILDO—*See* NECK-LOCK, 168 (note 2), 201.

DOUBLET—Down to *c.* 1660 the principal male body-garment, 2, 5, 29, 55, 121, 157, *2*, *3* A, *5*, *12*, *13*, *14* A, B, *24* B, *28* A, *48* B, *59*, *61*, *71* A, B, I. B, V. C, IX., XII. (*frontispiece*), XVI.–XXI., XXXI., XXXII. C, XXXIII A, XXXIV. D, XXXV., XXXIX., XL.

ÉCHELLE—Ladder-like trimming of graduated bows of ribbon across the opening of the bodice, 214, *81*, LVI.

297

FACINGS—Lapels.
FARTHINGALE—*See* VERDINGALE, 73, *50,*
  50bis, 52, XXIV., XXV., XXVII.–XXIX.
FOB—213, *96* B, *98, 103* A, LX. A.
FONTANGE, commode or tower—176,
  83 A, *87,* XLV. B.
FORE-PART—Inserted piece in front of a
  garment (*e.g.* a STOMACHER) to give the
  impression of a complete garment.
FORE-SLEEVE—One covering only the
  forearm.
FRENCH HOOD—281, *22,* XI.
FULL-BOTTOMED WIG—168, 199, *73, 75,*
  76 B, *78, 93,* XXXIX., XL., XLII., XLIII.,
  XLVI.–XLIX., LI. G, LIII. D.
FURBELOW (Fr. *falbala*)—174.

GABLE HOOD—23, 46, 281, *10* c., *11, 19, 21,*
  VIII.
GALLIGASKIN — Some kind of wide
  breeches ; *see* p. 62.
GALLOWSES—Braces, 282.
GLACÉ KID GLOVES—Explicitly described
  in Furetière's *Dictionnaire,* 1690, appar-
  ently introduced to Germany in 1685
  by Huguenot refugees, 186.
GLOVE-BANDS—137.
GUARDINFANTA—Late (seventeenth cen-
  tury) Spanish verdingale with enor-
  mously projecting hip. Cf. Velazquez'
  Las Meninas.

HAND-RUFF—Differs from the flat linen
  turned-up cuff as the RUFF does from the
  BAND ; *see also* RUFFLE, XV., XVI. A,
  XVII. A, XXIV.–XXVI., XXVIII., XXXII.
  B, D.
HANGERS (Pair of)—70, and note on p.
  83, *45.*
HEELS (in early inventories the term
  " high-heeled " means : reaching high
  up over the *wearer's* heel)—68, illustra-
  tions *passim.*
HÉRISSON—202, *92* B, C, *98.*
HOOP or PANIER—217, *104–111,* L.–LV.,
  LVII.–LIX.
HOSE—Originally a garment forming
  breeches and stockings in one, then
  signifies breeches alone and finally
  stockings only ; " round hose " and
  " French hose " are identical with or
  akin to TRUNK-HOSE (*q.v.*), 62.
HOUND'S EARS, or split cuffs with rounded
  corners, seventeenth and eighteenth
  centuries, *93, 94* B, XLIII., XLIX.
HURLUBERLU—185.

INTRODUCTION—ix.

JABOT—The double-frilled opening down
  the shirt front, 168, 212, *91, 95, 96,*
  L. G, LII. E.
JERKIN—Short coat worn over the doublet,
  2, 29, 57, 124, *24* A, C, *60,* II. B, IV. B, V. A, B,
  X., XI., XIII., XIV. B, XV. A, XXXIV. A.

KID GLOVES—*See* GLACÉ, 186.
KNUCKLE-BOW—Curved bar connecting
  the guard of a sword with the pummel,
  43, 45, XII., XIII., XV. A, XVII., XXI.

LEADING-STRINGS — Note on p. 187,
  XLVI. B.
LOCKET—*See* CHAPE.
LOVE-LOCK—A long lock of hair hanging
  in front of the ear, mostly plaited or
  beribboned, 67, 130, 169, *63* B.

MACCARONI, MACARONI—Note on p. 213,
  96, 100.
MAJOR WIG—297.
MANDILION—(1) Loose jerkin or frock
  with hanging sleeves, worn largely by
  soldiers ; (2) a similar livery coat for
  lackeys, sixteenth and seventeenth
  centuries, 57, *26.*
MANNISH MODES—175.
MONTERO—77, *77,* 165, 210.
MUFF—137, 170, 186, 213, 233, *76* B,
  112 A, *114* A, LI. A, G, LII. E.
MULE—185, 233, *94* A.

NECK-LOCK or DILDO—Small " corkscrew "
  curl at nape of periwig, 201, *89* B.
NETHER-STOCK—Early term for stocking
  or lower portion of hose.
NIVERNOIS HAT—210, *100.*

" OPEN " HOSE—A fashion of loose knee-
  breeches, somewhat like our " running
  shorts," 62, *35* B, XX.

PANES—Parallel bands of stuff, usually
  made by slashing the surface ; especially the longitudinal straps adorning
  the TRUNK-HOSE (*q.v.*), 62.
PANIER—217, *104–111,* L.–LV., LVII.–LIX.
PANTALOON-BREECHES—A term much used
  in England for PETTICOAT-BREECHES
  or RHINEGRAVE-BREECHES (*q.v.*).
PANTOFFLE—69, *42* C, XVI. A.
PARASOL—186, 233, *110* A, *115* B, *117* B.
PATCH—137, 186, 233.
PATTEN—*See* CLOG, 130, *66* B, C.
PATTERNS—269.
PEASECOD-BELLY—A fashionable distor-
  tion of the doublet or jerkin in front
  by means of bombast, busks, etc., 55,
  24, 33 C, XVII.
PETTICOAT-BREECHES or RHINEGRAVE-
  BREECHES, 160, *71* A, B, *73,* XXXIX.,
  XL. A.
PICKADIL, PICCADILLY—*See* notes on pp.
  30 and 80, XIII., XV. A.
PIGEON'S WING—201, *88, 94–95, 102,*
  L., LI.

INDEX AND GLOSSARY

PIGTAIL—200 and note at foot, *90 C, 91, 92 B, 100 E,* LI. A.

PINKING—A decoration of minute punctures in regular designs.

PLUDERHOSE—XV B., *34.*

POCKET (the first garments to be *lined with pockets* in the modern sense were the wide breeches of the sixteenth century).

POINT—Short, tagged lace or tie, xi, 8, 11, 13, 14, 17, 44, *8, 14, 19, 24, 32, 33 E, 59, 61, 66 A, 66 B,* VI., XXI., XXVII. A.

POKER or POKING-STICK—an instrument for " setting " the pleats of a ruff.

PORT-CANNONS—Hanging frills or valances of linen, lace, silk, etc., affixed below the knees of gentlemen (England, *c.* 1660–75), 162, *73,* XXXIX.

PULLINGS OUT—Material of lining puffed out limply through slashes.

PURITAN FASHIONS—132 (note).

QUEUE—199.

RAMILLIE WIG—200.

RAQUETTES or RATEPENADES—A fashion of dressing the front hair of women in two arches over a wire-frame, *c.* 1565–1590, *76, 77* (footnote), *48, 49,* XXV. B.

REBATO—Stiffened support for ruff or band.

REDINGOTE À L'ANGLAISE—Note on p. 247, *97.*

REÎTRE (MANTEAU À LA)—Long French cloak, often with a deep cape, 59, *28, 30.*

RHINEGRAVE—*See* PETTICOAT-BREECHES, 160, *71 A, B, 73,* XXXIX., XL. A.

ROBE À LA FRANÇAISE—216, *104, 115 C, D,* L. E, LII. C, LXIX.

ROBE À L'ANGLAISE—297.

ROLL—47.

ROSES (on shoes)—Hardly known before *c.* 1600.

RUFF or RUFF-BAND—Circular linen or lace collar of radiating tubular pleats, 67, *24, 28, 33, 37, 41, 44, 46, 49,* XIV., XV., XVI. A, XVII.–XX., XXXI., XXXIII. G, H, XXXVII. A.

RUFFLE—Originally = hand-ruff; later, any frill at the wrist, XV., XVI. A, XXIV.–XXVI., XXVIII., XXXII. B, D.

SACK—*See also* ROBE À LA FRANÇAISE, 216, *104, 115 C, D,* L. E, LII. C, LXIX.

SCABILONIANS, SCALINGS — Apparently same as CANIONS (*q.v.*).

SET or SETS—The pleats or gathers of a ruff, 67.

SHOULDER-BELT or BALDRICK—131, 169, *59–61, 71 B, 72–73, 75,* XL.

SIDE-PIECE (of a " pair of hangers ")—*45 a, a.*

SLASHING—Symmetrical slits in a garment, designed to show the lining, or under-garment, sixteenth and seventeenth centuries, 29 and illustrations *passim.*

SOLITAIRE—212, *88 B, D, 94–96, 102 A,* L. B, F, LI. B, C, J.

SPANISH BREECHES—296.

SPANISH CAPE—Shortish cloak with hanging cowl (so defined in Minsheu's Spanish-English Dictionary, sixteenth century, *s.v.* "*capa Castellana*"), 59, *27, 33 B,* LXIV. (fig. 2).

SPATTERDASH—166.

STARCH (coloured)—68 and footnote.

STEINKIRK—168, *78 C,* XLVI. E.

STOCK—212, *91, 95,* L. G.

STOMACHER—132, 214.

SUISSE (CHAPEAU À LA)—210, *99 A, B, 101 A,* LX. A.

SUPPORTASSE, SUPPORTER = REBATO (*q.v.*).

SURCOAT—*See* TUNIC.

TAURE—185, XLII.

THÉRÈSE—227, *125 A.*

TOUPET—199, 201, *92 A, 96 A, 100 B.*

TOURNURE—174, 218, *113 D, 116.*

TOWER—*See* FONTANGE.

TRUNK-HOSE (also TRUNKS and TRUNK-BREECHES)—Short, very wide breeches, commonly *bombasted* (*see under* BOMBAST) and *paned* (*see under* PANES), 60, *26 C, 32–33,* XII.–XIV., XVI., XIX.

TUNIC or SURCOAT—The name commonly given in England to the coat or *justau-corps* as first worn over the vest, *temp.* Charles II.

UPPER-STOCK—Early term for breeches, or upper portion of hose when of different material or design from the lower, 39.

VENETIANS—Early form of knee-breeches, 62, *27, 30,* XVII.

VERDINGALE, FARTHINGALE, 73, *50, 50bis, 52,* XXIV., XXV., XXVII.–XXIX.

VEST " after the Persian mode," p. ix, 158, and 296.

WAISTCOAT—Originally an *under-garment,* visible at most through the slashes of the doublet ; afterwards used in the modern sense.

"WATTEAU PLEAT" a misnomer, 216.

WHISK—68, *60, 130,* XXI.

WING—56, *121.*